italian

100 everyday recipes

First published in 2011
LOVE FOOD is an imprint of Parragon Books Ltd

Parragon
Queen Street House
4 Queen Street
Bath BA1 1HE, UK

ISBN: 978-1-4454-4285-3

Printed in China

Produced by Ivy Contract
Cover photography by Mike Cooper
Cover image home economy and food styling by Lincoln Jefferson

Notes for the Reader

This book uses both metric and imperial measurements. Follow the same units of measurement throughout; do not mix metric and imperial. All spoon measurements are level: teaspoons are assumed to be 5 ml, and tablespoons are assumed to be 15 ml. Unless otherwise stated, milk is assumed to be full fat, eggs and individual vegetables are medium, and pepper is freshly ground black pepper.

The times given are an approximate guide only. Preparation times differ according to the techniques used by different people and the cooking times may also vary from those given. Optional ingredients, variations or serving suggestions have not been included in the calculations.

Recipes using raw or very lightly cooked eggs should be avoided by infants, the elderly, pregnant women, convalescents and anyone suffering from an illness. Pregnant and breastfeeding women are advised to avoid eating peanuts and peanut products. Sufferers from nut allergies should be aware that some of the ready-made ingredients used in the recipes in this book may contain nuts. Always check the packaging before use.

Vegetarians should be aware that some of the prepared ingredients used in the recipes in this book may contain animal products. Always check the package before use.

italian

introduction

At the heart of Italian cuisine lies a very special ingredient – the legendary Italian love of good things, including good food. Learning the skills of cooking begins at an early age, as recipes and techniques are handed down the generations, and so too does an appreciation of well-prepared meals, whether a plate of al dente pasta topped with a simple sauce of freshly picked tomatoes, an aromatic beef stew or a perfect seafood risotto.

It is often said that the essence of Italian cooking can be summed up in two words – seasonal and regional. Italians respect their ingredients and insist on the best quality, so they prefer to use seasonal produce that, if possible, is locally grown. In provincial towns and villages, people shop daily for fresh produce in the markets and plan the menu for that day around whichever ingredients feel, smell and look to be in peak condition.

This emphasis has had a lasting effect on the style of Italian cuisine, and simplicity is the key word. But simplicity means something different in each region of Italy. The reason for this is a mix of geographical and cultural diversity. The north of the country is cooler and wetter, while the south is hotter and drier, and the crops reflect this. In the north, dairy farming produces butter, cream and cheese, which feature widely in the region's traditional cooking, and both rice and maize are cultivated here, so risotto and polenta are staples. The south, on the other hand, is the home of pasta, olives and olive oil, tomatoes, aubergines and citrus fruits.

The cultural differences arise from the fact that Italy has only relatively recently become a unified country, created from a number of independent states each with their own traditions, to which they adhere fiercely. This is perhaps part of the irresistible appeal of Italian cuisine – but whatever the reason, embrace it and enjoy it!

starters, soups & salads

artichokes with seafood

ingredients

serves 6

4–6 small young globe artichokes
juice of 2 lemons
60 ml/2 fl oz olive oil
3 garlic cloves, sliced
125 ml/4 fl oz white wine
450 g/1 lb frozen, pre-cooked
    mixed seafood (thawed)
300 g/10½ oz buffalo mozzarella,
    sliced
butter, for greasing
salt and pepper

method

1 Butter a baking dish. Clean the artichokes. Cut the stalks to a length of 4 cm/1½ inches, and peel. Remove the tough outer leaves and trim the inner leaves. Remove the hairy chokes.

2 Fill a bowl with 1 litre/1¾ pints of water and add the lemon juice. Cut the artichokes lengthways into thin slices and immediately drop them into the lemon water. Soak them for 10 minutes, then pour off the water and drain well.

3 Heat the olive oil in a non-stick frying pan and fry the garlic until it is golden brown, then remove and discard it.

4 Sauté the artichoke slices in the olive oil, stirring constantly. Season with salt and pepper, then add the white wine. Cover the pan and gently braise the artichokes on medium heat for about 30 minutes, shaking the pan several times as they cook.

5 Place the artichoke slices in the prepared dish and pour on the cooking juices. Add the seafood to the artichokes and top with mozzarella slices. Bake in a preheated oven, 200°C/400°F/Gas Mark 6, for 20 to 25 minutes until the mozzarella melts and starts to brown. Serve immediately.

country-style marinated aubergine slices

ingredients

serves 6

4 aubergines
6 tomatoes
2 garlic cloves
½ bunch parsley
60 ml/2 fl oz olive oil, plus
   extra for greasing
salt and pepper

method.

1 Wash and trim the aubergines, then cut into slices
   1 cm/½ inch thick. Sprinkle salt on them and place in
   a sieve to drain for 1 hour.

2 Meanwhile, peel and quarter the tomatoes, remove
   the seeds and finely dice the flesh. Peel the garlic and
   finely chop it along with the parsley. Add this mixture
   to the tomatoes, then season with salt and pepper to
   taste. Stir in 2 tablespoons of the olive oil and leave
   everything to marinate briefly.

3 Rinse and pat the aubergine slices dry with paper
   towels and arrange them next to each other on an
   oiled baking tray. Drizzle the remaining olive oil over
   them, then bake in a preheated oven, 200°C/400°F/
   Gas Mark 6, for 5 minutes on each side.

4 Brush the aubergine slices with the tomato mixture,
   stack them into little towers, and serve.

fennel salami carpaccio

ingredients

serves 4

2 large fennel bulbs
100 g/3½ oz fennel salami,
   finely sliced

dressing

juice of 1 lemon and 1 orange
1 tsp flower blossom honey
1 tsp mustard
1 tbsp white wine vinegar
60 ml/2 fl oz olive oil
salt and pepper

method

1 Trim the fennel and slice it very thinly with a mandolin
   or a food slicer. Decoratively arrange the sliced salami
   and fennel on 4 plates.

2 Whisk together the dressing ingredients and pour over
   the fennel salami carpaccio. Marinate for 10 minutes or
   longer before serving.

parma ham & figs

ingredients

serves 4

175 g/6 oz Parma ham,
    thinly sliced
4 fresh figs
1 lime
2 fresh basil sprigs
pepper

method

1 Using a sharp knife, trim the visible fat from the slices of Parma ham and discard. Arrange the Parma ham on four large serving plates, loosely folding it so that it falls into decorative shapes. Season to taste with pepper.

2 Using a sharp knife, cut each fig lengthways into 4 wedges. Arrange a fig on each serving plate. Cut the lime into 6 wedges, place a wedge on each plate and reserve the others. Remove the leaves from the basil sprigs and divide between the plates. Cover with clingfilm and chill in the refrigerator until ready to serve.

3 Just before serving, remove the plates from the refrigerator and squeeze the juice from the remaining lime wedges over the ham.

variation

Drizzle 3 tablespoons of balsamic vinegar and a little extra virgin olive oil over the salad.

prosciutto with rocket

ingredients

serves 4

115 g/4 oz rocket
1 tbsp lemon juice
3 tbsp extra virgin olive oil
225 g/8 oz prosciutto,
    thinly sliced
salt and pepper

method

1 Separate the rocket leaves, wash in cold water and pat dry on kitchen paper. Place the leaves in a bowl.

2 Pour the lemon juice into a small bowl and season to taste with salt and pepper. Whisk in the olive oil, then pour the dressing over the rocket leaves and toss lightly so they are evenly coated.

3 Carefully drape the prosciutto in folds on individual serving plates, then add the dressed rocket. Serve at room temperature.

chicken crostini

ingredients

serves 4

12 slices French bread
  or rustic bread
60 ml/2 fl oz olive oil
2 garlic cloves, chopped
2 tbsp finely chopped fresh
  oregano
100 g/3½ oz cold roast chicken,
  cut into small, thin slices
4 tomatoes, sliced
12 thin slices of goat's cheese
12 black olives, stoned and
  chopped
salt and pepper
fresh red and green salad leaves,
  to serve

method

1 Put the bread under a medium grill and lightly toast on both sides. Meanwhile, pour the olive oil into a bowl and add the garlic and oregano. Season with salt and pepper and mix well. Remove the toasted bread slices from the grill and brush them on one side only with the oil mixture.

2 Place the bread slices, oiled sides up, on a baking sheet. Put some sliced chicken on top of each one, followed by a slice of tomato. Divide the slices of goat's cheese between them, then top with the chopped olives.

3 Drizzle over the remaining oil mixture and transfer to a preheated oven, 180°C/350°F/Gas Mark 4. Bake for about 5 minutes, or until the cheese is golden and starting to melt. Remove from the oven and serve on a bed of fresh red and green salad leaves.

warm vegetable medley

ingredients

serves 6–8

60 ml/2 fl oz olive oil
2 celery sticks, sliced
2 red onions, sliced
450 g/1 lb aubergine, diced
1 garlic clove, finely chopped
5 plum tomatoes, chopped
3 tbsp red wine vinegar
1 tbsp sugar
3 tbsp green olives, stoned
2 tbsp capers
salt and pepper
ciabatta or panini, to serve

method

1 Heat half the olive oil in a large heavy-based saucepan. Add the celery and onions and cook over a low heat, stirring occasionally, for 5 minutes, until softened but not coloured. Add the remaining oil and the aubergine. Cook, stirring frequently, for about 5 minutes, until the aubergine starts to colour.

2 Add the garlic, tomatoes, vinegar and sugar, and mix well. Cover the mixture with a circle of waxed paper and simmer gently for about 10 minutes.

3 Remove the waxed paper, stir in the olives and capers and season to taste with salt and pepper. Pour the vegetables into a serving dish and set aside to cool to room temperature. Serve with ciabatta or panini.

sicilian stuffed tomatoes

ingredients

serves 4

8 large, ripe tomatoes
100 ml/3½ fl oz extra virgin
olive oil
2 onions, finely chopped
2 garlic cloves, crushed
115 g/4 oz fresh breadcrumbs
8 anchovy fillets in oil, drained
and chopped
3 tbsp black olives, stoned and
chopped
2 tbsp chopped fresh flat-leaf
parsley
1 tbsp chopped fresh oregano
115 g/4 oz freshly grated Parmesan
cheese

method

1 Cut a thin slice off the tops of the tomatoes and discard.
Scoop out the seeds with a teaspoon and discard,
taking care not to pierce the shells. Turn the tomato
shells upside down on kitchen paper to drain.

2 Heat 90 ml/3 fl oz of the olive oil in a frying pan, add
the onions and garlic and cook over a low heat, stirring
occasionally, for 5 minutes, until softened. Remove
the pan from the heat and stir in the breadcrumbs,
anchovies, olives and herbs.

3 Using a teaspoon, fill the tomato shells with the
breadcrumb mixture, then place in an ovenproof dish
large enough to hold them in a single layer. Sprinkle
the tops with grated Parmesan and drizzle with the
remaining oil.

4 Bake in a preheated oven, 180°C/350°F/Gas Mark 4,
for 20–25 minutes, until the tomatoes are tender and
the topping is golden brown.

5 Remove the dish from the oven and serve immediately,
if serving hot, or allow to cool to room temperature.

tuscan bean soup

ingredients

serves 4

140 g/5 oz dried white beans
100 g/3½ oz pancetta, or rindless
    smoked lean bacon
½ small green or savoy cabbage,
    thick stems removed and
    leaves shredded, cut into strips
2 carrots, sliced
400 g/14 oz canned peeled
    tomatoes
1 litre/1¾ pints meat stock
1 tbsp chopped fresh oregano
1 onion
4 slices day-old Tuscan
    country bread
55 g/2 oz grated Parmesan cheese
2 tbsp olive oil
salt and pepper

method

1 Soak the beans overnight in 1 litre/1¾ pints of water.
   The next day, bring to the boil in the soaking water
   and simmer for 1 hour, until tender.

2 Finely dice the pancetta. Add it to a large pan and
   gently cook until the fat starts to run. Sauté the
   cabbage and carrots in the fat. Mash the tomatoes
   with a fork and add them to the pan. Pour in the stock
   and season with the oregano and salt and pepper.

3 When the beans have cooked, pour off the cooking
   water, add the beans to the soup and simmer for
   another 15 minutes. Slice the onion into very thin rings.

4 Toast the bread, cut it in half and place in four
   ovenproof soup bowls. Pour the soup over the bread
   and top with onion rings. Sprinkle with Parmesan and
   drizzle with the olive oil. Bake in a preheated oven,
   200°C/400°F/Gas Mark 6, until the onion rings are
   golden brown. Serve immediately.

white bean soup

ingredients
serves 4

175 g/6 oz dried cannellini beans,
    soaked overnight in cold water
1.7 litres/3 pints chicken or
    vegetable stock
115 g/4 oz dried corallini,
    conchigliette piccole or other
    soup pasta
90 ml/3 fl oz olive oil
2 garlic cloves, finely chopped
salt and pepper

method

1 Drain the soaked beans and place them in a large
   heavy-based saucepan. Add the stock and bring to
   the boil. Partially cover the pan, reduce the heat and
   simmer for 2 hours, until tender.

2 Transfer about half the beans and a little of the stock to
   a food processor or blender and process to a smooth
   purée. Return the purée to the pan and stir well to mix.
   Bring the soup back to the boil.

3 Add the pasta to the soup, bring back to the boil and
   cook for 10 minutes, until tender.

4 Meanwhile, heat 4 tablespoons of the olive oil in a
   small saucepan. Add the garlic and cook over a low
   heat, stirring frequently, for 4–5 minutes, until golden.
   Stir the garlic into the soup. Season to taste with salt
   and pepper and ladle into warmed soup bowls. Drizzle
   with the remaining olive oil and serve immediately.

fresh tomato soup

ingredients

serves 4

1 tbsp olive oil
650 g/1 lb 7 oz plum tomatoes
1 onion, cut into quarters
1 garlic clove, thinly sliced
1 celery stick, roughly chopped
500 ml/18 fl oz chicken stock
55 g/2 oz dried anellini or other
   soup pasta
salt and pepper
fresh flat-leaf parsley, chopped,
   to garnish

method

1 Pour the olive oil into a large heavy-based saucepan and add the tomatoes, onion, garlic and celery. Cover and cook over a low heat for 45 minutes, occasionally shaking the pan gently, until the mixture is pulpy.

2 Transfer the mixture to a food processor or blender and process to a smooth purée. Push the purée through a sieve into a clean pan.

3 Add the stock and bring to the boil. Add the pasta, bring back to the boil and cook for 8–10 minutes, until the pasta is tender but still firm to the bite. Season to taste with salt and pepper. Ladle into warmed bowls, sprinkle with the parsley and serve immediately.

minestrone

ingredients

serves 4

3 tbsp olive oil

2 onions, chopped

½ small green or savoy cabbage,
thick stems removed and
leaves shredded

2 courgettes, chopped

2 celery sticks, chopped

2 carrots, chopped

2 potatoes, chopped

4 large tomatoes, peeled
and chopped

115 g/4 oz dried cannellini beans,
soaked overnight in cold water

1.2 litres/2 pints chicken or
vegetable stock

115 g/4 oz dried soup pasta

salt and pepper

freshly shaved Parmesan cheese,
to garnish

freshly grated Parmesan cheese,
to serve

method

1 Heat the oil in a large heavy-based saucepan. Add the onions and cook over a low heat, stirring occasionally, for 5 minutes, or until softened.

2 Add the cabbage, courgettes, celery, carrots, potatoes and tomatoes to the pan, cover and cook, stirring occasionally, for 10 minutes.

3 Drain and rinse the beans, then add to the pan. Pour in the stock, bring to the boil, cover and simmer for 1–1½ hours, or until the beans are tender.

4 Add the soup pasta to the pan and cook, uncovered, for 8–10 minutes, or until tender but still firm to the bite. Season to taste with salt and pepper and ladle into warmed bowls. Garnish with fresh Parmesan cheese shavings and an extra sprinkling of pepper. Serve immediately, handing around the grated Parmesan cheese separately.

orange salad

ingredients

serves 4

4 oranges
1 red onion
2 tbsp finely chopped parsley
60 ml/2 fl oz olive oil
salt and pepper

method

1 Peel the oranges and remove the pith, then slice in rounds. Lay them out in a fan pattern on a plate. Peel and halve the onion, and thinly slice one half. Finely chop the other and combine with the parsley.

2 Sprinkle the sliced and chopped onions over the orange slices, season with a little salt and pepper, and drizzle olive oil over the salad. Cover with clingfilm and marinate for 1 hour in the refrigerator. Remove from the refrigerator 5 minutes before serving.

pasta salad with chargrilled peppers

ingredients

serves 4

1 red pepper
1 orange pepper
280 g/10 oz dried conchiglie
75 ml/2½ fl oz extra virgin
    olive oil
2 tbsp lemon juice
1 garlic clove, finely chopped
3 tbsp shredded fresh
    basil leaves
salt

pesto

4 tbsp fresh basil leaves
1 tbsp pine kernels
1 garlic clove
25 g/1 oz freshly grated
    Parmesan cheese
3 tbsp extra virgin olive oil

method

1 Put the whole peppers on a baking sheet and place under a preheated grill, turning frequently, for 15 minutes, until charred all over. Remove with tongs and place in a plastic bag and set aside.

2 Meanwhile, make the pesto. Put the basil, pine kernels and garlic into a mortar and pound to a paste with a pestle. Transfer to a bowl and gradually work in the Parmesan with a wooden spoon, followed by the olive oil to make a thick, creamy sauce.

3 Bring a large saucepan of lightly salted water to the boil. Add the pasta, bring back to the boil and cook for 8–10 minutes, until tender but still firm to the bite.

4 Combine the olive oil, lemon juice, pesto and garlic in a bowl, whisking well to mix. Drain the pasta, add it to the pesto mixture while still hot and toss well. Set aside.

5 When the peppers are cool enough to handle, peel off the skins, then cut open and remove the seeds. Roughly slice the flesh and add it to the pasta with the basil and toss well. Serve at room temperature.

warm pasta salad

ingredients

serves 4

225 g/8 oz dried farfalle or other
    pasta shapes
6 pieces of sun-dried tomato in oil,
    drained and chopped
4 spring onions, chopped
55 g/2 oz rocket, shredded
½ cucumber, deseeded and diced
2 tbsp freshly grated Parmesan
    cheese
salt and pepper

dressing

60 ml/2 fl oz olive oil
½ tsp caster sugar
1 tbsp white wine vinegar
1 tsp Dijon mustard
4 fresh basil leaves, finely shredded
salt and pepper

method

1 To make the dressing, whisk the olive oil, sugar, vinegar and mustard together in a bowl. Season to taste with salt and pepper. Stir in the basil.

2 Bring a large heavy-based saucepan of lightly salted water to the boil. Add the pasta, return to the boil and cook for 8–10 minutes, or until tender but still firm to the bite. Drain and transfer to a salad bowl. Add the dressing and toss well.

3 Add the sun-dried tomatoes, spring onions, rocket and cucumber, season to taste with salt and pepper, and toss. Sprinkle with the Parmesan cheese and serve warm.

three-colour salad

ingredients

serves 4

280 g/10 oz buffalo mozzarella, drained and thinly sliced
8 plum tomatoes, sliced
20 fresh basil leaves
125 ml/4 fl oz extra virgin olive oil
salt and pepper

method

1 Arrange the cheese and tomato slices on 4 individual serving plates and season to taste with salt. Set aside in a cool place for 30 minutes.

2 Sprinkle the basil leaves over the salad and drizzle with the olive oil. Season with pepper and serve the salad immediately.

variation

Slice 2 ripe avocado pears and alternate with the mozzarella cheese and tomatoes in the salad.

mozzarella salad
with sun-dried tomatoes

ingredients

serves 4

140 g/5 oz sun-dried tomatoes
    in olive oil (drained weight),
    reserving the oil from the
    bottle
1 tbsp roughly shredded
    fresh basil
1 tbsp roughly chopped fresh
    flat-leaf parsley
1 tbsp capers, rinsed
1 tbsp balsamic vinegar
1 garlic clove, roughly chopped
extra olive oil, if necessary
100 g/3½ oz mixed salad leaves,
    such as oak leaf lettuce, baby
    spinach and rocket
500 g/1 lb 2 oz smoked
    mozzarella, sliced
pepper

method

1 Put the sun-dried tomatoes, basil, parsley, capers,
vinegar and garlic in a food processor or blender.
Measure the oil from the sun-dried tomatoes jar and
add in enough olive oil to make 150 ml/5 fl oz. Add
it to the food processor or blender and process until
smooth. Season to taste with pepper.

2 Divide the salad leaves between 4 individual serving
plates. Top with the slices of mozzarella and spoon the
dressing over them. Serve immediately.

meat & poultry

fillet of beef in laurel wreath

ingredients

serves 4

4 beef fillet steaks,
    250 g/9 oz each
4 tsp spicy mustard
12 fresh bay leaves
3 tbsp olive oil
1 tbsp peppercorns, coarsely
    crushed
60 ml/2 fl oz Italian brandy
salt

method

1 Brush the edges of the steaks with the mustard.
Place 3 bay leaves around each steak and secure
with kitchen twine. Season with salt.

2 Heat the olive oil in an ovenproof pan and thoroughly
brown the steaks on both sides, then cook in a
preheated oven, 130°C/265°F/Gas Mark ½, for
15 to 20 minutes.

3 Place the steaks on heated plates. Pour off the frying
fat and sprinkle the peppercorns in the pan. Pour
in the brandy, heat slightly, then flambé. Drizzle the
brandy sauce over the fillets and serve immediately.

grilled steak with tomatoes & garlic

ingredients

serves 4

3 tbsp olive oil, plus extra
    for brushing
700 g/1 lb 9 oz tomatoes,
    peeled and chopped
1 red pepper, deseeded
    and chopped
1 onion, chopped
2 garlic cloves, finely chopped
1 tbsp chopped fresh flat-leaf
    parsley
1 tsp dried oregano
1 tsp sugar
4 x 175-g/6-oz entrecôte
    or rump steaks
salt and pepper

method.

1 To make the sauce, place the oil, tomatoes, red pepper, onion, garlic, parsley, oregano and sugar in a heavy-based saucepan and season to taste with salt and pepper. Bring to the boil, reduce the heat and simmer for 15 minutes.

2 Meanwhile, trim any fat around the outsides of the steaks. Season each generously with pepper (but no salt) and brush with olive oil. Cook under a preheated grill or on a griddle according to taste: 2–3 minutes each side for rare; 3–4 minutes each side for medium and 4–5 minutes on each side for well done.

3 Transfer the steaks to warmed individual plates and spoon the sauce over them. Serve immediately.

spaghetti with meatballs

ingredients

serves 6

1 potato, diced
400 g/14 oz steak mince
1 onion, finely chopped
1 egg
4 tbsp chopped fresh flat-leaf
    parsley
plain flour, for dusting
75 ml/2½ fl oz virgin olive oil
400 ml/14 fl oz passata
2 tbsp tomato purée
400 g/14 oz dried spaghetti
6 fresh basil leaves, shredded
salt and pepper
freshly grated Parmesan cheese,
    to garnish

method

1 Place the potato in a small saucepan, add cold water to cover and a pinch of salt, and bring to the boil. Cook for 10–15 minutes, until tender, then drain. Either mash thoroughly with a potato masher or fork or pass through a potato ricer.

2 Combine the potato, steak, onion, egg and parsley in a bowl and season to taste with salt and pepper. Spread out the flour on a plate. With dampened hands, shape the meat mixture into walnut-size balls and roll in the flour. Shake off any excess.

3 Heat the oil in a heavy-based frying pan, add the meatballs and cook over a medium heat, stirring and turning frequently, for 8–10 minutes, until golden all over.

4 Add the passata and tomato purée and cook for 10 minutes, until the sauce is reduced and thickened.

5 Meanwhile, bring a large saucepan of lightly salted water to the boil. Add the pasta, bring back to the boil and cook for 8–10 minutes, until tender but still firm to the bite.

6 Drain well and add to the meatball sauce, tossing well to coat. Transfer to a warmed serving dish, garnish with the basil leaves and Parmesan and serve immediately.

spaghetti bolognese

ingredients

serves 4

2 tbsp olive oil
1 tbsp butter
1 small onion, finely chopped
1 carrot, finely chopped
1 celery stick, finely chopped
50 g/1¾ oz mushrooms, diced
225 g/8 oz fresh beef mince
75 g/2¾ oz unsmoked bacon
    or ham, diced
2 chicken livers, chopped
2 tbsp tomato purée
125 ml/4 fl oz dry white wine
½ tsp freshly grated nutmeg
300 ml/10 fl oz chicken stock
125 ml/4 fl oz double cream
450 g/1 lb dried spaghetti
salt and pepper
2 tbsp chopped fresh flat-leaf
    parsley, to garnish
freshly grated Parmesan cheese,
    to serve

method

1 Heat the olive oil and butter in a large saucepan over a medium heat. Add the onion, carrot, celery and mushrooms to the pan, then cook until soft. Add the beef and bacon to the pan and cook until the beef is evenly browned.

2 Stir in the chicken livers and tomato purée and cook for 2–3 minutes. Pour in the wine and season with salt, pepper and the nutmeg. Add the stock. Bring to the boil, then cover and simmer gently over a low heat for 1 hour. Stir in the cream and simmer, uncovered, until reduced.

3 Bring a large saucepan of lightly salted water to the boil. Add the pasta, return to the boil and cook until tender but still firm to the bite. Drain and transfer to a warmed serving dish.

4 Spoon the meat sauce over the pasta, garnish with the parsley and serve with the Parmesan cheese.

baked lasagne

ingredients

serves 4

2 tbsp olive oil
55 g/2 oz pancetta, chopped
1 clove garlic, chopped
1 onion, chopped
225 g/8 oz fresh beef mince
2 carrots, chopped
2 celery sticks, chopped
115 g/4 oz chopped mushrooms
pinch of dried organo
75 ml/5 tbsp red wine
150 ml/5 fl oz beef stock
1 tbsp sun-dried tomato paste
225 g/8 oz dried no-precook
    lasagne sheets
115 g/4 oz grated Parmesan cheese
salt and pepper
mixed salad, to serve

tomato sauce

2 tbsp olive oil
1 small onion, finely chopped
1 garlic clove, finely chopped
1 green pepper, chopped
225 g/8 oz tomatoes, chopped
1 tbsp tomato purée
1 tbsp soft brown sugar
salt and pepper

method

1 To make the tomato sauce, heat the olive oil in a saucepan. Add the onion, garlic and pepper and cook over a low heat, for 5 minutes, until softened. Add the tomatoes, tomato purée, sugar and season to taste with salt and pepper. Cover and simmer, for 30 minutes, until thickened. Set aside to cool until needed.

3 Heat the oil in a large saucepan. Add the pancetta and cook over a medium heat, stirring occasionally, for 2–3 minutes. Reduce the heat to low, add the garlic and onion and cook for 5 minutes, until softened.

3 Add the beef, increase the heat to medium and cook, stirring frequently and breaking it up with the spoon, for 8–10 minutes, until evenly browned. Stir in the carrots, celery and mushrooms and cook, stirring occasionally, for a further 5 minutes. Add the oregano, wine and stock and stir in the sun-dried tomato paste. Season to taste with salt and pepper. Bring to the boil, reduce the heat and simmer for 40 minutes.

4 Make alternating layers of the beef sauce, lasagne sheets and Parmesan in a large, rectangular ovenproof dish. Pour the tomato sauce over the top to cover completely. Bake in a preheated oven, 190°C/375°F/Gas Mark 5, for 30 minutes. Remove from the oven and leave to stand for 10 minutes, and serve with a mixed salad.

meatball surprise

ingredients

serves 8

500 g/1 lb 2 oz steak mince
500 g/1 lb 2 oz pork mince
2 garlic cloves, finely chopped
55 g/2 oz fresh breadcrumbs
50 g/1¾ oz freshly grated
    Parmesan cheese
1 tsp dried oregano
½ tsp ground cinnamon
grated rind and juice of 1 lemon
2 eggs, lightly beaten
150 g/5½ oz fontina cheese
90 ml/3 fl oz virgin olive oil
140 g/5 oz dried breadcrumbs
salt and pepper
parsley sprigs, to garnish
1 quantity of tomato sauce
    (see page 52), to serve

method

1 Make 1 quantity of tomato sauce and set aside.

2 Combine the steak, pork, garlic, fresh breadcrumbs, Parmesan, oregano, cinnamon and lemon rind in a bowl. Stir in the lemon juice and beaten eggs, season with salt and pepper and mix well. Knead the mixture with dampened hands, then shape into 16 balls.

3 Cut the fontina into 16 cubes and press 1 cube into each meatball, then reshape them to enclose the cheese completely.

4 Heat the olive oil in a large heavy-based frying pan. Meanwhile, spread out the dried breadcrumbs on a shallow plate and roll the meatballs in them to coat.

5 Add the meatballs to the frying pan and cook until golden brown all over. Transfer to an ovenproof dish using a slotted spoon and bake in a preheated oven, 180°C/350°F/Gas Mark 4, for 15–20 minutes, until cooked through. Serve immediately, garnished with parsley sprigs and accompanied by the tomato sauce.

pizzettes

ingredients

serves 6–8

40 g/1½ oz compressed
  fresh yeast, crumbled,
  or 2 sachets easy-blend
  dried yeast
½ tsp sugar
125 ml/4 fl oz lukewarm water
400 g/14 oz strong flour bread,
  plus extra for dusting
1 tsp salt
60 ml/2 fl oz olive oil, plus extra
  for greasing and drizzling
75 ml/2½ fl oz water

topping

500 g/1 lb 2 oz tomatoes
1 radicchio
100 g/3½ oz bacon, cut into strips
50 g/1¾ oz pine kernels

method

1 Put the yeast into a small bowl and sprinkle with the sugar. Add the lukewarm water, then stir to dissolve the yeast and sugar. Cover with a clean tea towel and prove in a warm spot for 30 minutes. Sift the flour into a large bowl. Make a hollow in the centre and pour the yeast mixture, salt, olive oil and water into it. Knead everything into a smooth, silky dough, then shape it into a ball. Dust the ball with a little flour, cover and set aside in a warm place to rise for about 1 hour or until doubled in volume.

2 Grease 2 baking sheets with olive oil. Peel and quarter the tomatoes, remove the seeds, and cut into small dice. Trim the radicchio and break it into bite-sized pieces.

3 Divide the dough into 12 equal pieces. Form each into a ball, flatten and place the rounds on the baking sheets as small pizzettes. Top with the diced tomato and bacon and drizzle on a little oil. Bake in a preheated oven, 200°C/400°F/Gas Mark 6, for 15 minutes, then sprinkle the radicchio and pine kernels over the small pizzettes and bake for another 5 minutes. Serve immediately.

stuffed veal cutlets with peperonata

ingredients

serves 4

2 pickled anchovy fillets

1 tbsp capers

1 garlic clove

1 small sprig each of rosemary
    and sage

3 tbsp olive oil

4 veal cutlets, 200 g/7 oz each

1 onion, finely chopped

salt and pepper

peperonata

2 each of red, green and yellow
    peppers, deeseeded

500 g/1 lb 2 oz tomatoes

1 tbsp olive oil

2 onions, finely chopped

2 garlic cloves, finely chopped

1 bay leaf

1 dried chilli, crumbled

3 tbsp balsamic vinegar

1 pinch sugar

1 small sprig rosemary

salt and pepper

method

1 To make the peperonata, cut the peppers into bite-size
   pieces. Roughly chop the tomatoes. Heat the olive oil
   in a large saucepan and sauté the onions. Add the
   peppers and garlic and gently simmer for 5 minutes.
   Add the tomatoes, bay leaf and chilli. Stir in the vinegar
   and sugar, cover and simmer for 15 minutes. Season
   to taste and add the rosemary. Pour into a jug and
   leave overnight.

2 Rinse and drain the anchovies and capers in a colander.
   Peel the garlic clove. Strip the rosemary leaves from
   the branch and pick the sage leaves. Place these
   ingredients in a mortar or blender, add pepper and
   1 tablespoon of the olive oil, and work into a paste.

3 Wash the meat and pat it dry. Using a sharp knife, cut
   a pocket horizontally into each cutlet. Stuff the pockets
   with the anchovy paste and secure with cocktail sticks.

4 Heat the remaining olive oil in a frying pan and brown
   the cutlets on both sides, then place in a baking dish.
   Sauté the onion in the pan. Add the peperonata, heat
   and spread over the meat. Season with salt and pepper
   and bake in a preheated oven, 160°C/325°F/Gas Mark 3,
   for 20 minutes. Serve.

veal with prosciutto & sage

ingredients

serves 4

4 veal escalopes
2 tbsp lemon juice
1 tbsp chopped fresh
    sage leaves
4 slices prosciutto
55 g/2 oz unsalted butter
3 tbsp dry white wine
salt and pepper

method

1 Place the veal escalopes between two sheets of clingfilm and pound with the flat end of a meat mallet or the side of a rolling pin until very thin. Transfer to a plate and sprinkle with the lemon juice. Set aside for 30 minutes, spooning the juice over them occasionally.

2 Pat the escalopes dry with kitchen paper, season with salt and pepper and rub with half the sage. Place a slice of prosciutto on each escalope and secure with a cocktail stick.

3 Melt the butter in a large heavy-based frying pan. Add the remaining sage and cook over a low heat, stirring constantly, for 1 minute. Add the escalopes and cook for 3–4 minutes on each side, until golden brown. Pour in the wine and cook for a further 2 minutes.

4 Transfer the escalopes to a warmed serving dish and pour the pan juices over them. Remove and discard the cocktail sticks and serve immediately.

pappardelle with rabbit sauce

ingredients

serves 4

4 rabbit legs
60 ml/2 fl oz olive oil
1 onion, finely diced
1 carrot, diced
1 celery stick, diced
250 ml/9 fl oz red wine
400 g/14 oz pappardelle
salt and pepper
1 tbsp finely chopped parsley,
    to garnish

method

1 Wash the rabbit legs, pat them dry, then vigorously rub them with salt and pepper.

2 Heat the olive oil in a flameproof casserole and sauté the diced vegetables. Add the rabbit legs and brown on both sides. Deglaze with the wine, cover and stew over a low heat for about 40 minutes, until the meat is done. Then take the legs out of the sauce. Remove the meat from the bones, cut it into small cubes and put the meat back into the sauce.

3 Bring a large saucepan of lightly salted water to the boil. Add the pasta and cook until al dente. Mix the drained pasta into the sauce and add salt and pepper to taste. Serve garnished with parsley.

cannelloni with spinach & ricotta

ingredients

serves 4

12 dried cannelloni tubes
butter, for greasing

filling

140 g/5 oz lean ham, chopped
140 g/5 oz frozen spinach,
   thawed and drained
115 g/4 oz ricotta cheese
1 egg
3 tbsp freshly grated Pecorino
   Romano cheese
pinch of freshly grated nutmeg
salt and pepper

cheese sauce

600 ml/1 pint milk
25 g/1 oz unsalted butter
1 oz/25 g plain flour
85 g/3 oz freshly grated Gruyère
   cheese
salt and pepper

method

1 Bring a large saucepan of lightly salted water to the boil.
   Add the cannelloni tubes, bring back to the boil, and
   cook for 6–7 minutes, until nearly tender. Drain and rinse
   under cold water. Spread the tubes on a clean tea towel.

2 Process the ham, spinach and ricotta in a food
   processor until combined. Add the egg and Pecorino
   and process to a smooth paste. Transfer the filling to
   a bowl, add the nutmeg and season to taste.

3 Grease an ovenproof dish with butter. Spoon the
   filling into a piping bag fitted with a 1-cm/¹/₂-inch
   nozzle. Carefully pipe the filling into the cannelloni
   tubes and place in the dish.

4 To make the cheese sauce, heat the milk to just below
   boiling point. Melt the butter in another saucepan.
   Stir in the flour and cook over a low heat, stirring
   constantly, for 1 minute. Gradually stir in the hot milk,
   then bring to the boil, stirring constantly. Simmer over
   a very low heat, stirring frequently, for 10 minutes, until
   thick and smooth. Remove the pan from the heat, stir
   in the Gruyère and season to taste.

5 Spoon the sauce over the filled cannelloni. Bake in a
   preheated oven, 180°C/350°F/Gas Mark 4, for 20–25
   minutes. Serve immediately.

spaghetti alla carbonara

ingredients

serves 4

450 g/1 lb dried spaghetti
1 tbsp olive oil
225 g/8 oz pancetta, or rindless
    smoked lean bacon, chopped
4 eggs
75 ml/2½ fl oz single cream
85 g/3 oz freshly grated
    Parmesan cheese
salt and pepper

method

1 Bring a large heavy-based saucepan of lightly salted water to the boil. Add the pasta, return to the boil and cook for 8–10 minutes, or until tender but still firm to the bite.

2 Meanwhile, heat the olive oil in a heavy-based frying pan. Add the chopped pancetta and cook over a medium heat, stirring frequently, for 8–10 minutes.

3 Beat the eggs with the cream in a small bowl and season to taste with salt and pepper. Drain the pasta and return it to the pan. Tip in the contents of the frying pan, then add the egg mixture and half the Parmesan cheese. Stir well, then transfer to a warmed serving dish. Serve immediately, sprinkled with the remaining Parmesan cheese.

variation

Add 25 g/1 oz mushrooms to the chopped pancetta and fry together in the olive oil.

sausages with borlotti beans

ingredients

serves 4

2 tbsp virgin olive oil
500 g/1 lb 2 oz luganega or other
    Italian sausages
140 g/5 oz smoked pancetta, or
    rindless smoked lean bacon,
    diced
2 red onions, chopped
2 garlic cloves, finely chopped
225 g/8 oz dried borlotti beans,
    soaked overnight in cold water
2 tsp finely chopped fresh
    rosemary
2 tsp chopped fresh sage
300 ml/10 fl oz dry white wine
salt and pepper
fresh rosemary sprigs,
    to garnish
crusty bread, to serve

method

1 Heat the oil in a flameproof casserole. Add the sausages
and cook over a low heat, turning frequently, for
10 minutes, or until browned all over. Remove from
the casserole and set aside.

2 Add the pancetta to the casserole, increase the heat to
medium and cook, stirring frequently, for 5 minutes, or
until golden brown. Remove with a slotted spoon and
set aside.

3 Add the onions to the casserole and cook over a low
heat, stirring occasionally, for 5 minutes, until softened.
Add the garlic and cook for a further 2 minutes.

4 Drain the beans and set aside the soaking liquid. Add
the beans to the casserole, then return the sausages
and pancetta. Gently stir in the herbs and pour in the
wine. Measure the reserved soaking liquid and add
300 ml/10 fl oz to the casserole. Season to taste with
salt and pepper. Bring to the boil over a low heat and
boil for 15 minutes, then transfer to a preheated oven,
140°C/275°F/Gas Mark 1, and cook for 2¾ hours.

5 Remove the casserole from the oven and ladle the
sausages and beans onto 4 warmed plates. Garnish
with the rosemary sprigs and serve immediately with
crusty bread.

sausage & rosemary risotto

ingredients

serves 4

2 long fresh rosemary sprigs,
    plus extra to garnish
2 tbsp olive oil
55 g/2 oz butter
1 large onion, finely chopped
1 celery stick, finely chopped
2 garlic cloves, finely chopped
½ tsp dried thyme leaves
450 g/1 lb pork sausages, such
    as luganega or Cumberland,
    cut into 1-cm/½-inch pieces
350 g/12 oz risotto rice
125 ml/4 fl oz fruity red wine
1.3 litres/2¼ pints simmering
    chicken stock
85 g/3 oz freshly grated
    Parmesan cheese
salt and pepper

method

1 Strip the long thin leaves from the rosemary sprigs and chop finely, then set aside.

2 Heat the oil and half the butter in a deep saucepan over a medium heat. Add the onion and celery and cook, stirring occasionally, for 2 minutes. Stir in the garlic, thyme, sausage and rosemary. Cook, stirring frequently, for 5 minutes, or until the sausage starts to brown. Transfer the sausage to a plate.

3 Reduce the heat and stir in the rice. Cook, stirring constantly, for 2–3 minutes, or until the grains are translucent.

4 Add the wine and cook, stirring, for 1 minute until reduced. Gradually add the hot stock, a ladleful at a time. Stir constantly and add more liquid as the rice absorbs each addition. Increase the heat to medium so that the liquid bubbles. Cook for 20 minutes, or until all the liquid is absorbed and the rice is creamy.

5 Towards the end of cooking, return the sausage pieces to the risotto and heat through. Season to taste. Remove from the heat and add the remaining butter. Mix well, then stir in the Parmesan until it melts. Spoon the risotto onto warmed plates, garnish with rosemary sprigs and serve.

spicy pork risotto

ingredients

serves 4

1 thick slice white bread, crust
   removed and discarded, soaked
   in water or milk for 5 minutes
450 g/1 lb pork mince
2 garlic cloves, minced
1 tbsp finely chopped onion
1 tsp black peppercorns,
   lightly crushed
1 egg
corn oil, for pan-frying
400 g/14 oz canned
   chopped tomatoes
1 tbsp tomato purée
1 tsp dried oregano
1 tsp fennel seeds
pinch of sugar
40 g/1½ oz butter
1 tbsp olive oil
1 small onion, finely chopped
280 g/10 oz risotto rice
150 ml/5 fl oz red wine
1 litre/1¾ pints simmering
   beef stock
salt and pepper
fresh basil leaves, to garnish

method

1 Drain the bread soaked in milk and squeeze to remove
   all the liquid. Mix the bread, pork, garlic, onion, crushed
   peppercorns and a pinch of salt together in a bowl.
   Add the egg and mix well.

2 Heat some corn oil in a frying pan over a medium
   heat. Form the meat mixture into balls and cook until
   browned. Remove each batch from the pan and drain.

3 Combine the tomatoes, tomato purée, oregano, fennel
   seeds and sugar in a heavy-based saucepan. Add the
   meatballs. Bring the sauce to the boil over a medium
   heat, then reduce the heat and simmer for 30 minutes.

4 Melt 25 g/1 oz of the butter with the olive oil in a
   deep saucepan over a medium heat. Stir in the onion
   and cook, stirring frequently, for 5 minutes, until soft.
   Reduce the heat and stir in the rice. Cook, stirring, for
   2–3 minutes, or until the grains are translucent. Add
   the wine and cook, stirring, for 1 minute until reduced.
   Gradually add the hot stock, stirring constantly until
   the liquid is absorbed and the rice is creamy. Season
   to taste.

5 Lift out the cooked meatballs and add to the risotto.
   Remove from the heat and stir in the remaining butter.
   Serve the risotto and meatballs drizzled with tomato
   sauce, and garnished with basil.

pork with fennel seeds & garlic

ingredients

serves 4

600 g/1 lb 5 oz lean pork

2–3 tbsp olive oil

1 tsp fennel seeds

5 garlic cloves, finely chopped

1 fresh red chilli, deseeded and
    finely chopped

300 g/10½ oz tomatoes,
    peeled and diced

salt and pepper

basil sprigs, to garnish

method

1 Wash the meat, pat it dry and cut into bite-sized pieces.
Heat the olive oil in a flameproof casserole, then add
the fennel seeds and garlic to it. Season the meat with
salt and pepper.

2 Brown the meat on all sides in the hot olive oil. As soon
as the meat browns, add the chilli and tomatoes. Cover
the pot and cook over low heat for about 1 hour,
adding a little warm water as needed. Serve the stew
immediately, garnished with basil sprigs.

variation

For a traditional Italian addition to the stew, add 55 g/2 oz
canned cannellini beans, drained and rinsed, to the pot
30 minutes before serving.

pepperoni pasta

ingredients

serves 4

3 tbsp olive oil
1 onion, finely chopped
1 red pepper, deseeded and diced
1 orange pepper, deseeded
    and diced
800 g/1 lb 12 oz canned
    chopped tomatoes
1 tbsp sun-dried tomato purée
1 tsp paprika
225 g/8 oz pepperoni, sliced
2 tbsp chopped fresh flat-leaf
    parsley, plus extra to garnish
450 g/1 lb dried garganelli
salt and pepper
mixed salad leaves, to serve

method

1 Heat 2 tablespoons of the olive oil in a large heavy-
based frying pan. Add the onion and cook over a
low heat, stirring occasionally, for 5 minutes, or until
softened. Add the red and orange peppers, tomatoes
and their can juices, sun-dried tomato purée and
paprika to the pan and bring to the boil.

2 Add the pepperoni and parsley and season to taste
with salt and pepper. Stir well and bring to the boil,
then reduce the heat and simmer for 10–15 minutes.

3 Meanwhile, bring a large heavy-based saucepan of
lightly salted water to the boil. Add the pasta, return
to the boil, and cook for 8–10 minutes, or until tender
but still firm to the bite. Drain well and transfer to a
warmed serving dish. Add the remaining olive oil
and toss. Add the sauce and toss again. Sprinkle with
parsley and serve immediately with mixed salad leaves.

roast lamb with rosemary & marsala

ingredients

serves 6

1.8 kg/4 lb leg of lamb
2 garlic cloves, thinly sliced
2 tbsp fresh rosemary leaves
120 ml/4 fl oz olive oil
900 g/2 lb potatoes, cut into
    2.5-cm/1-inch cubes
6 fresh sage leaves, chopped
150 ml/5 fl oz Marsala
salt and pepper

method

1 Use a small, sharp knife to make incisions all over the lamb, opening them out slightly to make little pockets. Insert the garlic slices and about half the rosemary leaves in the pockets.

2 Place the lamb in a roasting tin and spoon over half the olive oil. Roast in a preheated oven, 220°C/425°F/Gas Mark 7, for 15 minutes. Reduce the oven temperature to 180°C/350°F/Gas Mark 4. Remove the lamb from the oven and season to taste. Turn the lamb over, return to the oven and roast for a further 20 minutes.

3 Meanwhile, spread out the cubed potatoes in a second roasting tin, pour the remaining olive oil over them and toss to coat. Sprinkle with the remaining rosemary and the sage. Add the potatoes to the oven and roast with the lamb for 40 minutes.

4 Remove the lamb from the oven, turn it over and pour over the Marsala. Return it to the oven with the potatoes and cook for a further 15 minutes. Remove and cover with foil. Place the roasting tin over a high heat, bring to the boil and boil until thickened and syrupy. Strain into a warmed gravy boat or jug. Carve the lamb into slices and serve with the potatoes and sauce.

lamb shanks with roasted onions

ingredients

serves 4

4 x 350-g/12-oz lamb shanks,
   with any excess fat trimmed off
6 garlic cloves, each cut into
   slices lengthways
2 tbsp virgin olive oil
1 tbsp very finely chopped
   fresh rosemary
4 red onions
350 g/12 oz carrots, cut into
   thin sticks
60 ml/2 fl oz water
salt and pepper

method

1 Using a small, sharp knife, make incisions in each lamb shank. Insert garlic slices in each incision. Place the lamb in a single layer in a roasting pan, drizzle with the olive oil, sprinkle with the rosemary and season with pepper. Roast in a preheated oven, 180°C/350°F/Gas Mark 4, for 45 minutes.

2 Wrap each onion in a square of foil. Remove the lamb shanks from the oven and season with salt. Return the pan to the oven and place the onions on the shelf next to it. Roast for a further 1 hour, or until the lamb is tender.

3 Meanwhile, bring a large saucepan of water to the boil. Add the carrot sticks and blanch for 1 minute. Drain and refresh under cold water.

4 Remove the roasting tin from the oven and transfer the lamb to a warmed serving dish. Skim off any fat from the roasting tin and place over a medium heat. Add the carrots and cook for 2 minutes, then add the water, bring to the boil and simmer, stirring constantly and scraping up the glazed bits from the bottom of the tin.

5 Transfer the carrots and sauce to the serving dish. Remove the onions from the oven and unwrap. Cut and discard about 1 cm/½ inch off the tops of the onions and add the onions to the dish. Serve immediately.

barbecued chicken

ingredients

serves 4

1 maize-fed chicken, about
    1.2 kg/2 lb 10 oz
2 tsp grated lemon rind
3 garlic cloves, finely sliced
juice of 3 lemons
90 ml/3 fl oz olive oil
salt and pepper

method

1 Wash the chicken, pat it dry and cut it in half lengthways. Lay the chicken halves in a bowl and season them with pepper. Spread the lemon rind and garlic over the chicken. Pour on the lemon juice and olive oil, then cover and marinate overnight in the refrigerator.

2 The next day, take the chicken halves out of the marinade and drain. Season the meat with salt and barbecue slowly over charcoal or set under a medium grill until crisp on both sides and the juices run clear when a skewer is inserted into the thickest part of the meat. Brush the chicken occasionally with the marinade while grilling. Serve.

tuscan chicken

ingredients

serves 4

2 tbsp plain flour
4 skinned chicken quarters
    or portions
3 tbsp olive oil
1 red onion, chopped
2 garlic cloves, finely chopped
1 red pepper, deseeded
    and chopped
pinch of saffron threads
150 ml/5 fl oz chicken stock or a
    mixture of chicken stock and
    dry white wine
400 g/14 oz canned tomatoes,
    chopped
4 sun-dried tomatoes in oil,
    drained and chopped
225 g/8 oz mushrooms, sliced
115 g/4 oz black olives, stoned
60 ml/2 fl oz lemon juice
salt and pepper
fresh basil leaves, to garnish

method

1 Place the flour on a shallow plate and season with salt and pepper. Coat the chicken in the seasoned flour, shaking off any excess. Heat the olive oil in a large flameproof casserole. Add the chicken and cook over a medium heat, turning frequently, for 5–7 minutes, until golden brown. Remove from the casserole and set aside.

2 Add the onion, garlic and red pepper to the casserole, reduce the heat and cook, stirring occasionally, for 5 minutes, until softened. Meanwhile, stir the saffron into the stock.

3 Stir the tomatoes and their can juices, the sun-dried tomatoes, mushrooms and olives into the casserole and cook, stirring occasionally, for 3 minutes. Pour in the stock and saffron mixture and the lemon juice. Bring to the boil, then return the chicken pieces to the casserole.

4 Cover and cook in a preheated oven, 180°C/350°F/Gas Mark 4, for 1 hour, until the chicken is tender. Garnish with the basil leaves and serve immediately.

creamy chicken ravioli

ingredients

serves 4

115 g/4 oz cooked skinless,
boneless chicken breast,
roughly chopped

55 g/2 oz prosciutto, roughly
chopped

1 shallot, roughly chopped

55 g/2 oz ricotta cheese

55 g/2 oz freshly grated Pecorino
Romano cheese

pinch of freshly grated nutmeg

2 eggs, lightly beaten

1 quantity basic pasta dough
(see page 148, omitting the
spinach from the recipe)

plain flour, for dusting

salt and pepper

2 tbsp fresh basil, plus extra
to garnish

sauce

300 ml/10 fl oz double cream

2 garlic cloves, finely chopped

115 g/4 oz chestnut mushrooms,
thinly sliced

25 g/1 oz freshly grated Pecorino
Romano cheese

salt and pepper

method

1 Place the chicken, prosciutto and shallot in a food processor and process until chopped and blended. Transfer to a bowl and stir in the ricotta cheese and 25 g/1 oz of the Pecorino, the nutmeg and half the egg. Season to taste with salt and pepper.

2 Halve the pasta dough. Wrap one piece in clingfilm and thinly roll out the other on a lightly floured work surface. Cover with a tea towel and roll out the second piece of dough. Place small mounds of the filling in rows 4 cm/1½ inches apart on one sheet of dough and brush the spaces in between with beaten egg. Fit the second piece of dough on top. Press down firmly between the mounds of filling, pushing out any air. Cut into squares and let rest for 1 hour.

3 Bring a large saucepan of lightly salted water to the boil. Add the ravioli, in batches, return to the boil and cook for 5 minutes. Remove with a slotted spoon and drain on kitchen paper, then transfer to a warmed dish.

4 Meanwhile, to make the sauce, pour the cream into a frying pan, add the garlic and bring to the boil. Simmer for 1 minute, then add the mushrooms and half of the cheese. Season to taste and simmer for 3 minutes. Stir in the basil, then pour the sauce over the ravioli. Serve sprinkled with the remaining cheese and basil.

chicken tortellini

ingredients

serves 4

115 g/4 oz boneless chicken
    breast, skinless
55 g/2 oz prosciutto
40 g/1½ oz cooked spinach,
    well drained
1 tbsp finely chopped onion
55 g/2 oz freshly grated
    Parmesan cheese
pinch of ground allspice
1 egg, beaten
1 quantity basic pasta dough
    (see page 148, omitting the
    spinach from the recipe)
salt and pepper
2 tbsp chopped fresh parsley,
    to garnish

sauce

300 ml/10 fl oz single cream
2 garlic cloves, crushed
115 g/4 oz button mushrooms,
    thinly sliced
25 g/1 oz freshly grated
    Parmesan cheese
salt and pepper

method

1 Bring a pan of salted water to the boil. Add the chicken
and poach for about 10 minutes. Cool slightly, then
place in a food processor with the prosciutto, spinach
and onion and process until finely chopped. Stir in half
of the Parmesan cheese, allspice and egg and season
with salt and pepper to taste.

2 Thinly roll out the pasta dough and cut into 4–5-cm/
1½–2-inch circles.

3 Place ½ teaspoon of the chicken and ham filling in the
centre of each circle. Fold the pieces in half and press
the edges to seal, then wrap each piece round your
index finger, cross over the ends, and curl the rest of
the dough backward to make a navel shape. Re-roll the
trimmings and repeat until all of the dough is used up.

4 Bring a saucepan of salted water to the boil. Add the
tortellini, in batches, return to the boil and cook for
5 minutes. Drain well and transfer to a serving dish.

5 To make the sauce, bring the cream and garlic to the
boil in a small saucepan, then simmer for 3 minutes.
Add the mushrooms and the cheese, season to taste
with salt and pepper and simmer for 2–3 minutes.
Pour the sauce over the tortellini. Sprinkle over the
remaining Parmesan cheese, garnish with the parsley
and serve.

fish & seafood

sole with artichokes

ingredients

serves 1–2

8 small purple artichokes
juice of 1 lemon
125 ml/4 fl oz olive oil
4 garlic cloves, finely sliced
250 ml/9 fl oz dry white wine
400 ml/14 fl oz stock
800 g/1 lb 12 oz fillet of sole
salt
freshly ground pepper
flour for coating
1 tbsp finely chopped parsley

method

1 Clean the artichokes, then shorten the stalks to about 4 cm/1½ inches and peel them. Remove the tough outer leaves and trim the hard thorns from the remaining leaves. Mix the lemon juice and some water in a bowl. Slice the artichokes lengthways and immediately put them in the lemon water. Marinate for a short time, then pour off the liquid and pat the artichokes dry.

2 Heat 6 tablespoons of the olive oil in a large frying pan and sauté the artichokes. Add the garlic and sauté until golden brown. Deglaze with the wine, pour in the stock, and add salt and pepper. Simmer for 20 to 25 minutes, then remove from the stovetop.

3 Season the fish fillets with salt and pepper, coat in flour and shake off the excess. Heat the remaining oil and fry the fish on both sides. Serve the fish over the artichokes, sprinkled with the chopped parsley.

white fish stew

ingredients

serves 4

1 kg/2 lb 4 oz white fish, cleaned
    and gutted
2 tbsp olive oil
1 onion, finely chopped
2 garlic cloves, finely chopped
2 carrots, diced
2 celery sticks, diced
250 g/9 oz tomatoes, peeled
    and quartered, diced
500 ml/18 fl oz fish stock
2 bay leaves
1 tbsp balsamic vinegar
4 slices white bread
salt and pepper

method

1 Wash the fish, pat it dry and cut into bite-sized pieces.
Season with salt and pepper.

2 Heat the olive oil in a saucepan and sauté the onion
and garlic. Add the carrots and celery, browning lightly.
Mix in the tomatoes, pour in the fish stock and add the
bay leaves. Simmer together for 10 minutes.

3 Add the fish to the stew and cook on a low heat for
about 10 minutes. Remove the bay leaves and season
the stew with salt, pepper and the balsamic vinegar.
Toast the white bread and place each slice in a deep
bowl. Ladle the fish stew over the toast slices and
serve immediately.

fried anchovies

ingredients

serves 4

500 g/1 lb 2 oz anchovies (or
    sardines), as small as possible
flour, for coating
2 tbsp olive oil
coarse sea salt
1 lemon, to serve

method.

1 Wash the anchovies. If the fish are larger than 9 cm/
   3½ inches cut off and discard the heads. If they are
   smaller, you can use the entire fish. Coat the anchovies
   with flour and tap off the excess.

2 Heat the olive oil in a frying pan, add the fish and fry
   for a minute or so, turning them over to cook on both
   sides. Place the anchovies on a plate and sprinkle with
   coarse sea salt. Cut the lemon into quarters and serve
   with the anchovies.

seafood-stuffed artichokes

ingredients

serves 4

4 large globe artichokes
300 ml/10 fl oz water
3 tbsp lemon juice
60 ml/2 fl oz olive oil
1 small onion, finely chopped
2 garlic cloves, finely chopped
250 g/9 oz frozen, pre-cooked
    mixed seafood
2 tbsp finely chopped parsley
2 tbsp breadcrumbs
salt and pepper

method

1 Remove the stalks and leaves from the artichokes. Carefully remove the fuzzy choke from the inside with a spoon and wash the artichoke bases.

2 Combine the water with the lemon juice and a little salt in a saucepan and bring to the boil. Add the artichoke bases and simmer for 30 minutes, then set them upside down in a sieve to drain.

3 Heat 2 tablespoons of the olive oil in a frying pan and sauté the onion and garlic. Add the frozen seafood and cook until the thawing liquid has evaporated. Then remove from the heat, stir in the parsley, and season with salt and pepper. Stuff the artichoke bases with the seafood mixture.

4 Place the stuffed artichokes side by side in a baking dish, sprinkle with the breadcrumbs and drizzle with the remaining olive oil. Cook under a preheated grill until golden brown. Serve immediately.

trout fillets with mushrooms

ingredients

serves 4

8 trout fillets, gutted and boned
1 tbsp chopped fresh tarragon
500 ml/18 fl oz white wine
500 g/1 lb 2 oz porcini mushrooms
100 g/3½ oz butter
1 small onion, finely chopped
1 tbsp chopped fresh thyme
salt and pepper

method

1 Wash the trout fillets, pat them dry, and rub with salt and pepper. Place the fish in a bowl, sprinkle with the tarragon and pour 125 ml/4 fl oz wine over them. Cover the bowl and marinate for 30 minutes.

2 Meanwhile, wipe the mushrooms with a damp cloth, trim the stalks and cut them into 1-cm/½-inch thick slices. Heat half of the butter in a heavy-based frying pan and sauté the onion until translucent. Add the mushrooms and sauté while stirring until the liquid has evaporated. Pour in the rest of the wine and season with salt, pepper and the thyme. Simmer on a low heat for 10 minutes.

3 Melt the rest of the butter in a large, non-stick frying pan. Remove the trout fillets from the marinade, pat them dry and sauté in hot butter for 3 minutes on each side. Then pour in the marinade and bring it to the boil. Serve the mushrooms with the fish.

red mullet with capers & olives

ingredients

serves 4

700 g/1 lb 9 oz mullet fillets
(about 12)
3 tbsp chopped fresh marjoram
or flat-leaf parsley
thinly peeled rind of 1 orange,
cut into thin strips
225 g/8 oz mixed salad leaves,
torn into pieces
3 tbsp virgin olive oil
1 fennel bulb, cut into thin sticks
salt and pepper

dressing

175 ml/6 fl oz extra virgin
olive oil
1 tbsp balsamic vinegar
1 tbsp white wine vinegar
1 tsp Dijon mustard
salt and pepper

sauce

15 g/½ oz butter
40 g/1½ oz black olives, stoned
and thinly sliced
1 tbsp capers, rinsed

method

1 Place the fish fillets on a plate, sprinkle with the marjoram and season to taste. Set aside.

2 Blanch the orange rind in a small saucepan of boiling water for 2 minutes, drain, refresh under cold water and drain well again. Place the salad leaves in a large bowl.

3 To make the dressing, whisk together the extra virgin olive oil, vinegars and mustard in a small bowl and season to taste. Pour the dressing over the salad leaves and toss well. Arrange the salad leaves on a large serving platter to make a bed.

4 Heat the virgin olive oil in a large heavy-based frying pan. Add the fennel and cook, stirring constantly, for 1 minute. Remove the fennel with a slotted spoon, set aside and keep warm. Add the fish fillets, skin-side down, and cook for 2 minutes. Carefully turn them over and cook for a further 1–2 minutes. Remove from the pan and drain on kitchen paper. Keep warm.

5 To make the sauce, melt the butter in a small saucepan, add the olives and capers and cook, stirring constantly, for 1 minute.

6 Place the fish fillets on the bed of salad leaves, top with the orange rind and fennel and pour over the sauce. Serve immediately.

swordfish with olives & capers

ingredients

serves 4

2 tbsp plain flour
4 x 225-g/8-oz swordfish steaks
100 ml/3½ fl oz olive oil
2 garlic cloves, halved
1 onion, chopped
4 anchovy fillets, drained and
    chopped
4 tomatoes, peeled, deseeded
    and chopped
12 green olives, stoned and sliced
1 tbsp capers, rinsed
salt and pepper
fresh rosemary leaves, to garnish

method

1 Spread out the flour on a plate and season with salt
  and pepper. Coat the fish in the seasoned flour,
  shaking off any excess.

2 Gently heat the olive oil in a large heavy-based frying
  pan. Add the garlic and cook over a low heat for
  2–3 minutes, until just golden. Do not let it turn brown
  or burn. Remove the garlic and discard.

3 Add the fish to the pan and cook over a medium heat
  for about 4 minutes on each side, until cooked through
  and golden brown. Remove the fish from the pan and
  set aside.

4 Add the onion and anchovies to the pan and cook,
  mashing the anchovies with a wooden spoon until
  they have turned to a purée and the onion is golden.
  Add the tomatoes and cook over a low heat, stirring
  occasionally, for about 20 minutes, until the mixture
  has thickened.

5 Stir in the olives and capers and taste and adjust the
  seasoning. Return the steaks to the pan and heat
  through gently. Serve garnished with rosemary.

grilled sardines with lemon sauce

ingredients

serves 4

1 large lemon
85 g/3 oz unsalted butter
20 fresh sardines, cleaned and
    heads removed
1 tbsp chopped fresh fennel
    leaves
salt and pepper

method

1 Peel the lemon. Remove all the bitter pith and discard. Using a small, serrated knife, cut between the membranes and ease out the flesh segments, discarding any seeds. Chop finely and set aside.

2 Melt 2 tablespoons of the butter in a small saucepan and season with salt and pepper. Brush the sardines all over with the melted butter and cook under a preheated grill or on a barbecue, turning once, for 5–6 minutes, until cooked through.

3 Meanwhile, melt the remaining butter, then remove the pan from the heat. Stir in the chopped lemon and fennel.

4 Transfer the sardines to a warmed platter, pour the sauce over them and serve immediately.

linguine with anchovies, olives & capers

ingredients

serves 4

3 tbsp olive oil

2 garlic cloves, finely chopped

10 anchovy fillets, drained and chopped

140 g/5 oz black olives, stoned and chopped

1 tbsp capers, rinsed

450 g/1 lb plum tomatoes, peeled, deseeded and chopped

pinch of cayenne pepper

400 g/14 oz dried linguine

salt

2 tbsp chopped fresh flat-leaf parsley, to garnish

method

1 Heat the olive oil in a heavy-based saucepan. Add the garlic and cook over a low heat, stirring frequently, for 2 minutes. Add the anchovies and mash them to a pulp with a fork. Add the olives, capers and tomatoes and season to taste with cayenne pepper. Cover and simmer for 25 minutes.

2 Meanwhile, bring a pan of lightly salted water to the boil. Add the pasta, bring back to the boil and cook for 8–10 minutes, until tender but still firm to the bite. Drain and transfer to a warmed serving dish.

3 Spoon the anchovy sauce into the dish and toss the pasta, using two large forks. Garnish with the parsley and serve immediately.

sicilian tuna

ingredients

serves 4

4 x 140-g/5-oz tuna steaks
2 fennel bulbs, thickly sliced
    lengthways
2 red onions, sliced
2 tbsp virgin olive oil
crusty rolls, to serve

marinade

125 ml/4 fl oz extra virgin olive oil
4 garlic cloves, finely chopped
4 fresh red chillies, deseeded and
    finely chopped
juice and finely grated rind of
    2 lemons
3 tbsp finely chopped fresh
    flat-leaf parsley
salt and pepper

method

1 First, make the marinade by whisking all the ingredients together in a bowl. Place the tuna steaks in a large shallow dish and spoon over 3 tablespoons of the marinade, turning to coat. Season to taste, cover and leave for 30 minutes. Set aside the remaining marinade.

2 Heat a ridged griddle pan. Put the fennel and onions in a bowl, add the oil and toss well to coat. Add to the griddle pan and cook for 5 minutes on each side, until just starting to colour. Transfer to four warmed serving plates, drizzle with the reserved marinade and keep warm.

3 Add the tuna steaks to the griddle pan and cook, turning once, for 4–5 minutes, until firm to the touch but still moist inside. Transfer the tuna to the plates and serve immediately with crusty rolls.

beans with tuna

ingredients

serves 4

800 g/1 lb 12 oz cannellini beans,
    soaked overnight in cold water
90 ml/3 fl oz extra virgin olive oil
2 x 200-g/7-oz tuna steaks
2 garlic cloves, lightly crushed
sprig of fresh sage
2 tbsp water
salt and pepper
4 chopped fresh sage leaves,
    to garnish

method

1 Drain the soaked beans and place them in a saucepan.
Add enough water to cover and bring to the boil and
boil for 10 minutes. Reduce the heat and simmer for
1–1½ hours, until tender. Drain the beans thoroughly.

2 Heat 1 tablespoon of the olive oil in a heavy-based
frying pan. Add the tuna steaks and cook over a
medium heat for 3–4 minutes on each side, until
tender. Remove from the pan and set aside to cool.

3 Heat 3 tablespoons of the remaining olive oil in a
heavy-based frying pan. Add the garlic and sage sprig
and cook briefly over a low heat until the sage starts
to sizzle. Remove the garlic and discard.

4 Add the beans and cook for 1 minute, then add the
water and season to taste with salt and pepper. Cook
until the water has been absorbed. Remove and
discard the sage sprig, transfer the beans to a bowl
and set aside to cool.

5 Meanwhile, flake the tuna, removing any bones.
When the beans are lukewarm or at room temperature,
according to taste, gently stir in the tuna. Drizzle with
the remaining olive oil, sprinkle with the chopped sage
and serve.

seafood omelette

ingredients

serves 3

25 g/1 oz unsalted butter
1 tbsp olive oil
1 onion, very finely chopped
175 g/6 oz courgette, halved
    lengthways and sliced
1 celery stick, very finely chopped
85 g/3 oz button mushrooms,
    sliced
55 g/2 oz French beans, cut into
    5-cm/2-inch lengths
4 eggs
85 g/3 oz mascarpone cheese
1 tbsp chopped fresh thyme
1 tbsp shredded fresh basil
200 g/7 oz canned tuna, drained
    and flaked
115 g/4 oz cooked peeled prawns
salt and pepper

method

1 Melt the butter with the olive oil in a heavy-based frying pan with a flameproof handle. If the pan has a wooden handle, protect it with foil because it needs to go under the grill. Add the onion and cook over a low heat, stirring occasionally, for 5 minutes, until softened.

2 Add the courgette, celery, mushrooms and beans and cook, stirring occasionally, for a further 8–10 minutes, until starting to brown.

3 Beat the eggs with the mascarpone, thyme, basil, and salt and pepper to taste.

4 Add the tuna to the pan and stir it into the mixture with a wooden spoon, then add the prawns.

5 Pour the egg mixture into the pan and cook for 5 minutes, until it is just starting to set. Draw the egg from the sides of the pan towards the centre to let the uncooked egg run underneath.

6 Put the pan under a preheated grill and cook until the egg is just set and the surface is starting to brown. Cut the omelette into wedges and serve.

tuna with garlic, lemon, capers & olives

ingredients

serves 4

350 g/12 oz dried gnocchi
60 ml/2 fl oz olive oil
50 g/2 oz butter
3 large garlic cloves, thinly sliced
200 g/7 oz canned tuna, drained
    and broken into chunks
2 tbsp lemon juice
1 tbsp capers, drained
10–12 black olives, stoned
    and sliced
salt and pepper
2 tbsp chopped fresh
    flat-leaf parsley, to serve

method

1 Cook the gnocchi following the instructions on the packet until al dente. Drain and return to the saucepan.

2 Heat the olive oil and half the butter in a frying pan over a medium–low heat. Add the garlic and cook for a few seconds, or until just beginning to colour. Reduce the heat to low. Add the tuna, lemon juice, capers and olives. Stir the mixture gently until all the ingredients are heated through.

3 Transfer the gnocchi to a warm serving dish and pour the tuna mixture over the gnocchi. Add the parsley and remaining butter and season to taste. Toss the gnocchi well to mix and serve immediately.

risotto with tuna & pine kernels

ingredients

serves 4

85 g/3 oz butter
60 ml/2 fl oz olive oil
1 small onion, finely chopped
280 g/10 oz risotto rice
1.2 litres/2 pints simmering fish
  or chicken stock
225 g/8 oz tuna, canned
  and drained, or grilled
  fresh steaks
8–10 black olives, stoned
  and sliced
1 small pimiento, thinly sliced
1 tsp finely chopped
  fresh parsley
1 tsp finely chopped
  fresh marjoram
2 tbsp white wine vinegar
55 g/2 oz pine kernels
1 garlic clove, chopped
225 g/8 oz fresh tomatoes, peeled,
  deseeded and diced
85 g/3 oz freshly grated Parmesan
  or Grana Padano cheese
salt and pepper

method

1 Melt 2 tablespoons of the butter with 1 tablespoon of the oil in a deep saucepan over a medium heat. Add the onion and cook, stirring occasionally, until soft and starting to turn golden. Reduce the heat, add the rice and mix to coat in the oil and butter. Cook, stirring constantly, until the grains are translucent. Add the hot stock, a ladleful at a time, stirring constantly, until all the liquid is absorbed and the rice is creamy. Season to taste with salt and pepper.

2 While the risotto is cooking, flake the tuna into a bowl and mix in the olives, pimiento, parsley, marjoram and vinegar. Season with salt and pepper.

3 Heat the remaining oil in a small frying pan over a high heat. Add the pine kernels and garlic. Cook, stirring constantly, for 2 minutes, or until they just start to brown. Add the tomatoes and mix well. Continue cooking over a medium heat for 3–4 minutes or until they are thoroughly warm. Pour the tomato mixture over the tuna mixture and mix. Fold into the risotto 5 minutes before the end of the cooking time.

4 Remove the risotto from the heat when all the liquid has been absorbed and add the remaining butter. Mix well, then stir in the Parmesan until it melts. Serve the risotto immediately.

bavettine with smoked salmon & rocket

ingredients

serves 4

350 g/12 oz dried bavettine
or linguine
2 tbsp olive oil
1 garlic clove, finely chopped
115 g/4 oz smoked salmon,
cut into thin strips
55 g/2 oz rocket
salt and pepper
½ lemon, to garnish

method

1 Bring a large heavy-based saucepan of lightly salted water to the boil. Add the pasta, return to the boil and cook for 8–10 minutes, or until tender but still firm to the bite.

2 Just before the end of the cooking time, heat the olive oil in a heavy-based frying pan. Add the garlic and cook over a low heat, stirring constantly, for 1 minute. Do not allow the garlic to brown or it will taste bitter. Add the salmon and rocket. Season to taste with salt and pepper and cook, stirring constantly, for 1 minute. Remove the pan from the heat.

3 Drain the pasta and transfer to a warmed serving dish. Add the smoked salmon and rocket mixture, toss lightly and serve, garnished with a lemon half.

layered spaghetti with smoked salmon & prawns

ingredients

serves 6

350 g/12 oz dried spaghetti
70 g/2½ oz butter, plus extra
  for greasing
200 g/7 oz smoked salmon,
  cut into strips
280 g/10 oz large jumbo prawns,
  cooked, peeled and deveined
115 g/4 oz freshly grated Parmesan
  cheese

béchamel sauce

25 g/1 oz butter
1 tbsp plain flour
350 ml/12 fl oz warm milk
salt and pepper

method

1 To make the béchamel sauce, melt the butter in a saucepan over a low heat. Add the flour and stir with a wooden spoon. Turn the heat up a little and continue stirring for 2 minutes. Add half of the milk and stir to make a smooth paste. Add the remaining milk, stirring until you have a smooth, white sauce. Season with salt and pepper.

2 Bring a large saucepan of lightly salted water to the boil. Add the pasta, bring back to the boil and cook for 8–10 minutes, until tender but still firm to the bite. Drain well, return to the pan, add 4 tablespoons of the butter and toss well.

3 Butter a large ovenproof dish. Spoon half the spaghetti into the prepared dish, cover with the strips of smoked salmon, then top with the prawns. Pour over half the béchamel sauce and sprinkle with half the Parmesan. Add the remaining spaghetti, cover with the remaining sauce and sprinkle with the remaining Parmesan. Dice the remaining butter and dot it over the surface.

4 Bake in a preheated oven, 180°C/350°F/Gas Mark 4, for 15 minutes, until the top is golden. Serve immediately.

springtime pasta

ingredients

serves 4

2 tbsp lemon juice
4 baby globe artichokes
125 ml/4 fl oz olive oil
2 shallots, finely chopped
2 garlic cloves, finely chopped
2 tbsp chopped fresh flat-leaf
    parsley
2 tbsp chopped fresh mint
350 g/12 oz dried rigatoni or
    other tubular pasta
12 large raw prawns
25 g/1 oz unsalted butter
salt and pepper

method

1 Fill a bowl with cold water and add the lemon juice. Prepare the artichokes one at a time. Cut off the stems and trim away any tough outer leaves. Cut across the tops of the leaves. Slice in half lengthways and remove the central fibrous chokes, then cut lengthways into 5-mm/¼-inch thick slices. Place the slices in the bowl of acidulated water to prevent discoloration.

2 Heat 100 ml/3½ fl oz of the olive oil in a heavy-based frying pan. Drain the artichoke slices and pat dry with kitchen paper. Add them to the pan with the shallots, garlic, parsley and mint, and cook over a low heat, stirring frequently, for 10–12 minutes until tender.

3 Meanwhile, bring a large saucepan of lightly salted water to the boil. Add the pasta, bring back to the boil and cook for 8–10 minutes, until tender but firm.

4 Peel the prawns, cut a slit along the back of each and remove and discard the dark vein. Melt the butter in a small frying pan, cut the prawns in half and add them to the pan. Cook, stirring occasionally, for 2–3 minutes, until they have changed colour. Season to taste.

5 Drain the pasta and pour it into a bowl. Add the remaining olive oil and toss well. Add the artichoke mixture and the prawns and toss again. Serve the pasta immediately.

scallops with porcini & cream sauce

ingredients

serves 4

25 g/1 oz dried porcini
mushrooms
500 ml/18 fl oz hot water
3 tbsp olive oil
40 g/1½ oz butter
350 g/12 oz sliced scallops
2 garlic cloves, very finely
chopped
2 tbsp lemon juice
250 ml/9 fl oz double cream
350 g/12 oz dried fettuccine
or pappardelle
salt and pepper
2 tbsp chopped fresh
flat-leaf parsley, to serve

method

1 Put the porcini and hot water in a bowl and soak for 20 minutes. Strain the mushrooms, reserving the soaking water, and chop roughly. Line a sieve with kitchen paper and strain the mushroom water into a bowl.

2 Heat the oil and butter in a large frying pan over a medium heat. Add the scallops and cook for 2 minutes, or until just golden. Add the garlic and mushrooms, then stir-fry for another minute.

3 Stir in the lemon juice, cream and 150 ml/5 fl oz of the mushroom water. Bring to the boil, then simmer over a medium heat for 2–3 minutes, stirring constantly, until the liquid is reduced by half. Season with salt and pepper. Remove from the heat.

4 Meanwhile, bring a large saucepan of lightly salted water to the boil. Add the pasta, bring back to the boil and cook for 8–10 minutes, until tender but firm. Drain and transfer to a warm serving dish. Briefly reheat the sauce and pour over the pasta. Sprinkle with the parsley and toss well to mix. Serve immediately.

saffron & lemon risotto with scallops

ingredients

serves 4

16 scallops
juice of 1 lemon, plus extra
    for seasoning
40 g/1½ oz butter
1 tbsp olive oil, plus extra
    for brushing
1 small onion, finely chopped
280 g/10 oz risotto rice
1 tsp crumbled saffron threads
1.2 litres/2 pints simmering fish
    or vegetable stock
2 tbsp vegetable oil
115 g/4 oz freshly grated Parmesan
    or Grana Padano cheese
salt and pepper
1 lemon, cut into wedges
2 tsp lemon zest, to garnish

method

1 Place the scallops in a non-metallic bowl and mix with the lemon juice. Cover the bowl with clingfilm and chill in the refrigerator for 15 minutes.

2 Melt 1 tablespoon of the butter with the olive oil in a saucepan over a medium heat. Add the onion and cook, stirring occasionally, until soft. Add the rice and mix to coat in oil and butter. Cook until the grains are translucent. Dissolve the saffron in 4 tablespoons of hot stock and add to the rice. Add the remaining stock, stirring constantly, until all the liquid is absorbed and the rice is creamy. Season with salt and pepper.

3 When the risotto is nearly cooked, heat a griddle pan over a high heat. Brush the scallops with oil and sear on the griddle pan for 3–4 minutes on each side, depending on their thickness. Take care not to overcook or they will be rubbery.

4 Remove the risotto from the heat and add the remaining butter. Mix well, then stir in the Parmesan until it melts. Season with lemon juice, adding just 1 teaspoon at a time and tasting as you go. Serve the risotto immediately with the scallops and lemon wedges arranged on top, sprinkled with lemon zest.

seafood pizza

ingredients

serves 2

plain flour, for dusting
olive oil, for oiling and drizzling
1 quantity tomato sauce
    (see page 52)
225 g/8 oz mixed fresh seafood
½ red pepper and ½ yellow pepper,
    deseeded and chopped
1 tbsp capers, rinsed
55 g/2 oz Taleggio cheese, grated
3 tbsp freshly grated Parmesan
    cheese
½ tsp dried oregano
75 g/2¾ oz anchovy fillets in oil,
    drained and sliced
10 black olives, stoned
salt and pepper

pizza dough

225 g/8 oz plain flour, plus
    extra for dusting
1 tsp salt
1 tsp easy-blend dried yeast
1 tbsp olive oil
90 ml/3 fl oz lukewarm water

method

1 To make the pizza dough, sift the flour and salt into
a bowl and stir in the yeast. Make a well in the centre
and pour in the oil and water. Incorporate the dry
ingredients into the liquid, using floured hands.

2 Turn out the dough onto a lightly floured work surface
and knead well for 5 minutes, until smooth and elastic.
Return to the clean bowl, cover with lightly oiled
clingfilm and set aside to rise in a warm place for
about 1 hour, or until doubled in size.

3 Turn out the dough again onto a lightly floured work
surface and knock down. Knead briefly, then roll out
the dough into a circle about 5 mm/¼ inch thick.
Transfer to a lightly oiled baking sheet and push up
the edge with your fingers to form a small rim.

4 Spread the tomato sauce over the pizza base, almost
to the edge. Arrange the mixed seafood, red and
yellow peppers and capers evenly on top.

5 Sprinkle the cheeses and oregano evenly over the
topping. Add the anchovy fillets and olives, drizzle
with olive oil. Season to taste with salt and pepper.

6 Bake in a preheated oven, 220°C/425°F/Gas Mark 7, for
20–25 minutes, until the crust is crisp and the cheese
has melted. Serve immediately.

vegetable dishes

sweet-and-sour pumpkin

ingredients

serves 4

125 ml/4 fl oz olive oil
750 g/1 lb 10 oz pumpkin flesh,
    cut into pieces
1 garlic clove, finely chopped
1 cinnamon stick
2 cloves
1 tbsp brown sugar
200 ml/7 fl oz mild white wine
    vinegar
10 basil leaves
salt and pepper

method

1 Heat the olive oil in a deep frying pan. Add the pumpkin and garlic and sauté. Season with salt and pepper, then add the cinnamon stick and cloves. Cook on a low heat, stirring occasionally, for 30 minutes; the pumpkin should still be firm to the bite.

2 When the pumpkin has cooked, remove the cinnamon and cloves from the pan. Season to taste with the sugar and vinegar. Cut the basil into fine strips and stir in. Serve the pumpkin hot or cold.

spinach in gorgonzola sauce

ingredients

serves 4

1 kg/2 lb 4 oz leaf spinach
55 g/2 oz butter
freshly grated nutmeg
125 ml/4 fl oz milk
125 ml/4 fl oz white wine
125 g/4½ oz mild Gorgonzola
2 egg yolks
salt and pepper

method

1 Thoroughly wash the spinach, removing any wilted leaves and coarse stalks.

2 Melt half the butter in a large saucepan. Add the spinach while it is still dripping wet and wilt it. Season with salt, pepper and nutmeg and keep warm on a low heat.

3 In a saucepan, simmer the milk and wine to reduce slightly. Crumble the Gorgonzola into the pan and melt it, stirring constantly. Remove from the heat. Whisk the egg yolks with a little of the sauce, then add it to the rest of sauce and fold in the spinach. Adjust the seasoning with salt and pepper and serve.

spicy broad beans

ingredients

serves 2

2 tbsp olive oil

4 shallots, finely sliced

2 garlic cloves, finely chopped

2 fresh chillies, halved and
    deseeded

250 ml/9 fl oz vegetable stock

400 g/14 oz fresh broad beans,
    shelled

2 sprigs savory

1 bay leaf

2 tomatoes, peeled, deseeded
    and diced

100 g/3½ oz pancetta, or rindless
    smoked lean bacon, finely
    diced

1 tbsp finely chopped fresh parsley

salt and pepper

method

1 Heat the olive oil in a frying pan and fry the shallots,
garlic and chillies. Pour in the vegetable stock and
bring to the boil. Add the beans, savory and bay leaf,
cover the pan and simmer for about 30 minutes.

2 Remove the herbs, stir in the tomatoes and season to
taste with salt and pepper.

3 In an ungreased frying pan, fry the pancetta until it is
crisp. Stir the pancetta and parsley into the vegetables
and serve.

rosemary potatoes

ingredients

serves 4

750 g/1 lb 10 oz potatoes, peeled
    and cut into cubes
3 garlic cloves, roughly chopped
3 sprigs rosemary, chopped
75 ml/2½ fl oz olive oil,
    plus extra for greasing
salt and pepper

method

1 Grease a flat baking dish with olive oil. Place a layer
of potatoes on the base of the baking dish. Season
with some of the garlic and rosemary, salt and pepper.
Repeat this procedure until all the ingredients have
been used. Drizzle the olive oil over the top.

2 Bake in a preheated oven, 200°C/400°F/Gas Mark 6, for
about 45 minutes, tossing the potatoes several times.
Serve in the baking dish while hot.

aubergines with mozzarella & parmesan

ingredients

serves 6–8

3 aubergines, thinly sliced
olive oil, for brushing
300 g/10½ oz buffalo mozzarella,
    sliced
115 g/4 oz freshly grated
    Parmesan cheese
3 tbsp dried breadcrumbs
15 g/½ oz butter
sprigs of fresh flat-leaf parsley,
    to garnish

tomato and basil sauce

2 tbsp virgin olive oil
4 shallots, finely chopped
2 garlic cloves, finely chopped
400 g/14 oz canned tomatoes
1 tsp sugar
8 fresh basil leaves, shredded
salt and pepper

method

1 Arrange the aubergine slices in a single layer on one or two lightly oiled large baking sheets. Brush with olive oil and bake in a preheated oven, 200°C/400°F/Gas Mark 6, for 15–20 minutes, until tender but not collapsing.

2 Meanwhile, make the tomato and basil sauce. Heat the oil in a heavy-based saucepan, add the shallots and cook, stirring occasionally, for 5 minutes, until softened. Add the garlic and cook for 1 minute more. Add the tomatoes and break them up with a wooden spoon. Stir in the sugar and season to taste with salt and pepper. Bring to the boil, reduce the heat and simmer for about 10 minutes, until thickened. Stir in the basil leaves.

3 Brush an ovenproof dish with olive oil and arrange half the aubergine slices in the bottom. Cover with half the mozzarella, spoon over half the tomato sauce and sprinkle with half the Parmesan. Mix the remaining Parmesan with the breadcrumbs. Repeat the layers, ending with the Parmesan mixture.

4 Dot the top with butter and bake for 25 minutes, until the topping is golden brown. Remove from the oven and leave to stand for 5 minutes before serving, garnished with the parsley.

aubergine & tomato bake

ingredients

serves 4

600 g/1 lb 5 oz aubergine,
    cut into 1-cm/$\frac{1}{2}$-inch
    thick slices
salt
225 ml/8 fl oz olive oil
600 g/1 lb 5 oz plum tomatoes,
    cut into 1-cm/$\frac{1}{2}$-inch
    thick slices
55 g/2 oz freshly grated
    Parmesan cheese
2 tbsp fresh white breadcrumbs
pepper

method

1 To remove any bitterness, layer the aubergine slices
   in a colander, sprinkling each layer with salt. Stand the
   colander in the sink and drain for 30 minutes. Meanwhile,
   spread out the tomato slices on kitchen paper, cover
   with more kitchen paper and drain. Rinse the aubergine
   thoroughly under cold running water to remove all
   traces of the salt, then pat dry with kitchen paper.

2 Heat 2 tablespoons of the olive oil in a large heavy-
   based frying pan. Add the tomato slices and cook for
   just 30 seconds on each side. Transfer to a large platter
   and season to taste with salt and pepper.

3 Wipe out the frying pan with kitchen paper, then
   add 2 tablespoons of the remaining olive oil and heat.
   Add the aubergine slices, in batches, and cook on
   both sides until golden brown. Remove from the pan
   and drain on kitchen paper. Cook the remaining slices
   in the same way, adding more olive oil as required.

4 Brush a large ovenproof dish with some of the
   remaining olive oil. Arrange alternate layers of
   aubergine and tomatoes, sprinkling each layer with
   Parmesan cheese. Top with the breadcrumbs and
   drizzle with the remaining olive oil. Bake in a preheated
   oven, 180°C/350°F/Gas Mark 4, for 25–30 minutes,
   until golden. Serve immediately.

spinach & ricotta dumplings

ingredients

serves 4

1 kg/2 lb 4 oz fresh spinach, washed and coarse stalks removed
350 g/12 oz ricotta cheese
115 g/4 oz freshly grated Parmesan cheese
3 eggs, lightly beaten
pinch of freshly grated nutmeg
115–175 g/4–6 oz plain flour, plus extra for dusting
salt and pepper

herb butter

115 g/4 oz unsalted butter
2 tbsp chopped fresh oregano
2 tbsp chopped fresh sage

method

1 Wash the spinach, place it in a saucepan with just the water clinging to its leaves, cover and cook over a low heat for 6–8 minutes, until just wilted. Drain well and set aside to cool.

2 Squeeze out as much liquid as possible from the spinach, then chop finely. Place the spinach in a bowl, add the ricotta, half the Parmesan, the eggs and nutmeg, season to taste and beat until thoroughly combined. Sift most of the flour into the mixture and lightly work it in, adding more if necessary, to make a workable mixture. Cover with clingfilm and chill in the refrigerator for 1 hour.

3 With floured hands, break off small pieces of the mixture and roll them carefully into walnut-sized balls – they are quite delicate. Dust the dumplings with flour.

4 Bring a large saucepan of lightly salted water to the boil. Add the dumplings and cook for 2–3 minutes, until they rise to the surface. Remove them from the pan with a slotted spoon, drain well and set aside.

5 To make the herb butter, melt the butter in a large heavy-based frying pan. Add the oregano and sage and cook over a low heat, stirring frequently, for 1 minute. Add the dumplings and toss gently to coat. Serve sprinkled with the remaining Parmesan.

spinach & ricotta ravioli

ingredients

serves 4

350 g/12 oz fresh spinach leaves, washed and coarse stalks removed
225 g/8 oz ricotta cheese
55 g/2 oz freshly grated Parmesan cheese
2 eggs, lightly beaten
pinch of freshly grated nutmeg
salt and pepper
freshly grated Parmesan cheese, to serve

spinach pasta dough

175 g/6 oz plain flour, plus extra for dusting
salt
225 g/8 oz frozen spinach, thawed, squeezed dry and finely chopped
2 eggs, lightly beaten
1 tbsp olive oil

method

1 To make the pasta dough, sift the flour into a food processor and add the salt. Add the chopped spinach, then pour in the eggs and olive oil and process until the dough begins to come together. Turn out onto a lightly floured work surface and knead until smooth. Wrap in clingfilm and set aside for at least 30 minutes.

2 Cook the spinach over a low heat for 5 minutes, until wilted. Drain and squeeze out as much moisture as possible. Cool, then chop finely. Beat the ricotta cheese until smooth, then stir in the spinach, Parmesan and half the egg. Season to taste with nutmeg and pepper.

3 Halve the pasta dough. Cover one piece and thinly roll out the other on a floured work surface. Cover and roll out the second piece. Put small mounds of filling in rows 4 cm/1½ inches apart on one sheet of dough and brush the spaces in between with the remaining beaten egg. Lay the second piece of dough on top. Press down between the mounds, pushing out any air. Cut into squares and rest on a tea towel for 1 hour.

4 Bring a large saucepan of salted water to the boil, add the ravioli, in batches, return to the boil, and cook for 5 minutes. Remove with a slotted spoon and drain on kitchen paper. Season to taste and serve with grated Parmesan cheese.

vegetarian lasagne

ingredients

serves 4

olive oil, for brushing
2 aubergines, sliced
25 g/1 oz butter
1 garlic clove, finely chopped
4 courgettes, sliced
1 tbsp finely chopped fresh
    flat-leaf parsley
1 tbsp finely chopped fresh
    marjoram
225 g/8 oz mozzarella cheese,
    grated
400 g/14 oz strained canned
    tomatoes
175 g/6 oz dried lasagne
1 quantity béchamel sauce
    (see page 122)
55 g/2 oz freshly grated
    Parmesan cheese
salt and pepper

method

1 Brush a large ovenproof dish with olive oil. Brush a large griddle pan with olive oil and heat until smoking. Add half the aubergine slices and cook over a medium heat for 8 minutes, or until golden brown all over. Remove the aubergine from the griddle pan and drain on kitchen paper. Add the remaining aubergine slices and extra oil, if necessary, and cook for 8 minutes, or until golden brown all over.

2 Melt the butter in a frying pan and add the garlic, courgettes, parsley and marjoram. Cook over a medium heat, stirring frequently, for 5 minutes, or until the courgettes are golden brown all over. Remove from the pan and let drain on kitchen paper.

3 Layer the aubergine, courgettes, mozzarella, strained tomatoes and lasagne in the dish, seasoning with salt and pepper as you go and finishing with a layer of lasagne. Pour over the béchamel sauce, making sure that all the pasta is covered. Sprinkle with the grated Parmesan cheese and bake in a preheated oven, 200°C/400°F/Gas Mark 6, for 30–40 minutes, or until golden brown. Serve the lasagne immediately.

mixed vegetable agnolotti

ingredients

serves 4

butter, for greasing
1 quantity basic pasta dough
    (see page 148, omitting the
    spinach from the recipe)
plain flour, for dusting
85 g/3 oz freshly grated
    Parmesan cheese
mixed salad leaves, to serve

filling

125 ml/4 fl oz olive oil
1 red onion, chopped
3 garlic cloves, chopped
2 large aubergines, cut into chunks
3 large courgettes, cut into chunks
6 beefsteak tomatoes, peeled,
    deseeded and roughly chopped
1 large green pepper, deseeded
    and diced
1 large red pepper, deseeded
    and diced
1 tbsp sun-dried tomato purée
1 tbsp shredded fresh basil
salt and pepper

method

1 To make the filling, heat the olive oil in a large heavy-based saucepan. Add the onion and garlic and cook over a low heat, stirring occasionally, for 5 minutes, or until softened. Add the aubergines, courgettes, tomatoes, green and red peppers, sun-dried tomato purée and basil. Season to taste with salt and pepper, cover and simmer gently, stirring occasionally, for 20 minutes.

2 Lightly grease an ovenproof dish with butter. Roll out the pasta dough on a lightly floured work surface and stamp out 7.5-cm/3-inch circles with a plain cutter. Place a spoonful of the vegetable filling on one side of each circle. Dampen the edges slightly and fold the pasta circles over, pressing together to seal.

3 Bring a large pan of lightly salted water to the boil. Add the agnolotti, in batches if necessary, return to the boil and cook for 3–4 minutes. Remove with a slotted spoon, drain and transfer to the dish. Sprinkle with the Parmesan cheese and bake in a preheated oven, 200°C/400°F/Gas Mark 6, for 20 minutes. Serve with salad leaves.

penne in a creamy mushroom sauce

ingredients

serves 4

50 g/2 oz butter
1 tbsp olive oil
6 shallots, sliced
450 g/1 lb chestnut
    mushrooms, sliced
1 tsp plain flour
150 ml/5 fl oz double cream
2 tbsp port
115 g/4 oz sun-dried tomatoes
    in oil, drained and chopped
pinch of freshly grated nutmeg
350 g/12 oz dried penne
salt and pepper
2 tbsp chopped fresh flat-leaf
    parsley, to garnish

method

1 Melt the butter with the olive oil in a large heavy-based frying pan. Add the shallots and cook over a low heat, stirring occasionally, for 4–5 minutes, or until softened. Add the mushrooms and cook over a low heat for a further 2 minutes. Season to taste with salt and pepper, sprinkle in the flour and cook, stirring, for 1 minute.

2 Remove the pan from the heat and gradually stir in the cream and port. Return to the heat, add the sun-dried tomatoes and grated nutmeg and cook over a low heat, stirring occasionally, for 8 minutes.

3 Meanwhile, bring a large heavy-based saucepan of lightly salted water to the boil. Add the pasta, return to the boil and cook for 8–10 minutes, or until tender but still firm to the bite. Drain the pasta well and add to the mushroom sauce. Cook for 3 minutes, then transfer to a warmed serving dish. Sprinkle with the parsley and serve immediately.

baked pasta with mushrooms

ingredients

serves 4

2 quantities of béchamel sauce
(see page 122)

140 g/5 oz fontina cheese,
thinly sliced

85 g/3 oz butter, plus extra
for greasing

350 g/12 oz mixed exotic
mushrooms, sliced

350 g/12 oz dried tagliatelle

2 egg yolks

115 g/4 oz freshly grated
pecorino cheese

salt and pepper

mixed salad greens, to serve

method

1 Make a double quantity of béchamel sauce. Stir the fontina cheese into the béchamel sauce and set aside.

2 Melt 2 tablespoons of the butter in a large saucepan. Add the mushrooms and cook over a low heat, stirring occasionally, for 10 minutes.

3 Meanwhile, bring a large saucepan of lightly salted water to the boil. Add the pasta, bring back to the boil and cook for 8–10 minutes, until tender but still firm to the bite. Drain, return to the pan and add the remaining butter, the egg yolks and about one third of the béchamel sauce, then season to taste. Toss well to mix, then gently stir in the mushrooms.

4 Lightly grease a large ovenproof dish and spoon in the pasta mixture. Pour over the remaining sauce evenly and sprinkle with the pecorino. Bake in a preheated oven, 200°C/400°F/Gas Mark 6, for 15–20 minutes, until golden brown. Serve immediately with mixed salad greens.

mushroom cannelloni

ingredients

serves 4

12 dried cannelloni tubes
25 g/1 oz butter
450 g/1 lb mixed wild mushrooms,
    finely chopped
1 garlic clove, finely chopped
85 g/3 oz fresh breadcrumbs
150 ml/5 fl oz milk
60 ml/2 fl oz olive oil, plus
    extra for brushing
225 g/8 oz ricotta cheese
115 g/4 oz freshly grated
    Parmesan cheese
2 tbsp pine kernels
2 tbsp flaked almonds
salt and pepper

tomato olive sauce

2 tbsp olive oil
1 onion, finely chopped
1 garlic clove, finely chopped
800 g/1 lb 12 oz canned
    chopped tomatoes
1 tbsp tomato purée
8 black olives, stoned and
    chopped
salt and pepper

method

1 Bring a large saucepan of lightly salted water to the boil. Add the cannelloni tubes, return to the boil and cook for 8–10 minutes, or until tender but still firm. With a slotted spoon, transfer the cannelloni tubes to a plate and pat dry.

2 Meanwhile, make the tomato olive sauce. Heat the olive oil in a frying pan. Add the onion and garlic and cook over a low heat for 5 minutes, or until softened. Add the tomatoes and their can juices, tomato purée and olives and season to taste. Bring to the boil and cook for 3–4 minutes. Pour the sauce into a large ovenproof dish brushed with olive oil.

3 To make the filling, melt the butter in a heavy-based frying pan. Add the mushrooms and garlic and cook over a medium heat, stirring frequently until tender. Remove the pan from the heat. Mix the breadcrumbs, milk and olive oil together in a large bowl, then stir in the ricotta, mushroom mixture and 85 g/3 oz of the Parmesan cheese. Season to taste with salt and pepper.

4 Fill the cannelloni tubes with the mushroom mixture and place them in the dish. Brush with olive oil and sprinkle with the remaining Parmesan cheese, pine kernels and almonds. Bake in a preheated oven, 190°C/375°F/Gas Mark 5, for 25 minutes, or until golden.

spaghetti with roasted garlic & pepper sauce

ingredients

serves 4

6 large garlic cloves, unpeeled
400 g/14 oz bottled roasted red
    peppers, drained and sliced
200 g/7 oz canned chopped
    tomatoes
3 tbsp olive oil
¼ tsp dried chilli flakes
1 tsp chopped fresh thyme
    or oregano
350 g/12 oz dried spaghetti,
    bucatini or linguine
salt and pepper
freshly grated Parmesan,
    to serve

method

1 Place the unpeeled garlic cloves in a shallow, ovenproof dish. Roast in a preheated oven, 200°C/400°F/Gas Mark 6, for 7–10 minutes, or until the cloves feel soft.

2 Put the peppers, tomatoes and oil in a food processor or blender, then purée. Squeeze the garlic flesh into the purée. Add the chilli flakes and oregano. Season with salt and pepper. Blend again, then scrape into a saucepan and set aside.

3 Bring a large heavy-based saucepan of lightly salted water to the boil. Add the pasta, return to the boil and cook for 8–10 minutes, or until tender but still firm to the bite. Drain and transfer to a warm serving dish.

4 Reheat the sauce and pour over the pasta. Toss well to mix. Serve immediately with Parmesan.

asparagus & sun-dried tomato risotto

ingredients

serves 4

1 tbsp olive oil
40 g/1½ oz butter
1 small onion, finely chopped
6 sun-dried tomatoes, thinly sliced
280 g/10 oz risotto rice
150 ml/5 fl oz dry white wine
1 litre/1¾ pints simmering
   vegetable stock
225 g/8 oz fresh asparagus
   spears, cooked
85 g/3 oz freshly grated Parmesan
   or Grana Padano cheese
salt and pepper
thinly grated lemon zest,
   to garnish

method

1 Heat the olive oil with 2 tablespoons of the butter in a deep saucepan over a medium heat until the butter has melted. Stir in the onion and sun-dried tomatoes and cook, stirring occasionally, for 5 minutes, until the onion is soft and starting to turn golden. Do not brown.

2 Reduce the heat, add the rice and mix to coat in the oil and butter. Cook, stirring constantly, for 2–3 minutes, or until the grains are translucent. Add the wine and cook, stirring constantly, until it has reduced.

3 Gradually add the hot stock, a ladleful at a time, stirring constantly, until all the liquid is absorbed and the rice is creamy. Season to taste with salt and pepper.

4 While the risotto is cooking, cut most of the asparagus into pieces about 2.5 cm/1 inch long. Keep several spears whole for garnishing the finished dish. Carefully fold the cut pieces of asparagus into the risotto for the last 5 minutes of cooking time.

5 Remove the risotto from the heat and add the remaining butter. Mix well, then stir in the Parmesan until it melts. Spoon the risotto onto individual warmed serving dishes and garnish with the whole spears of asparagus. Sprinkle over the lemon zest and serve.

risotto primavera

ingredients

serves 6–8

225 g/8 oz fresh thin asparagus
    spears
60 ml/2 fl oz olive oil
175 g/6 oz young green beans,
    cut into 2.5-cm/1-inch lengths
175 g/6 oz young courgettes,
    quartered and cut into
    2.5-cm/1-inch lengths
225 g/8 oz shelled fresh peas
1 onion, finely chopped
1–2 garlic cloves, finely chopped
350 g/12 oz risotto rice
1.5 litres/2¾ pints simmering
    vegetable stock
4 spring onions, cut into
    2.5-cm/1-inch lengths
55 g/2 oz butter
115 g/4 oz freshly grated
    Parmesan cheese
2 tbsp snipped fresh chives
2 tbsp shredded fresh basil
salt and pepper

method

1 Trim the woody ends of the asparagus and cut off the tips. Cut the stems into 2.5-cm/1-inch pieces and set aside with the tips.

2 Heat 2 tablespoons of the oil in a large frying pan over a high heat. Add the asparagus, beans, courgettes and peas and stir-fry for 3–4 minutes, until they are bright green and just starting to soften. Set aside.

3 Heat the remaining oil in a large heavy-based saucepan over a medium heat. Add the onion and cook, for 3 minutes, or until it starts to soften. Stir in the garlic and cook, stirring, for 30 seconds.

4 Reduce the heat, add the rice and mix to coat in oil. Cook, stirring constantly, for 2–3 minutes, or until the grains are translucent. Gradually add the hot stock, a ladleful at a time, until all but 2 tablespoons of the liquid is absorbed and the rice is creamy.

5 Stir in the stir-fried vegetables, onion mixture and spring onions with the remaining stock. Cook for 2 minutes, stirring frequently, then season to taste with salt and pepper. Stir in the butter, Parmesan, chives and basil.

6 Remove the pan from the heat. Transfer the risotto to a warmed serving dish and serve immediately.

wild mushroom risotto

ingredients

serves 6

55 g/2 oz dried porcini or morel
    mushrooms
about 500 g/1 lb 2 oz mixed fresh
    wild mushrooms, such as
    porcini, field mushrooms and
    chanterelles, halved if large
60 ml/2 fl oz olive oil
3–4 garlic cloves, finely chopped
55 g/2 oz butter
1 onion, finely chopped
350 g/12 oz risotto rice
50 ml/2 fl oz dry white vermouth
1.2 litres/2 pints simmering
    vegetable stock
115 g/4 oz freshly grated
    Parmesan cheese
3 tbsp chopped fresh
    flat-leaf parsley
salt and pepper

method

1 Place the dried mushrooms in a heatproof bowl
   and add boiling water to cover. Set aside to soak for
   30 minutes, then carefully lift out and pat dry. Strain
   through a sieve lined with kitchen paper and set aside.

2 Trim the fresh mushrooms and gently brush clean.
   Heat 3 tablespoons of the oil in a large frying pan.
   Add the fresh mushrooms and stir-fry for 1–2 minutes.
   Add the garlic and the soaked mushrooms and cook,
   stirring frequently, for 2 minutes. Transfer to a plate.

3 Heat the remaining oil and half the butter in a large
   heavy-based saucepan. Add the onion and cook over
   a medium heat, stirring occasionally, for 2 minutes,
   until softened. Reduce the heat, stir in the rice and
   cook, stirring constantly, for 2–3 minutes, until the
   grains are translucent. Add the vermouth and cook,
   stirring, for 1 minute until reduced.

4 Gradually add the hot stock, a ladleful at a time,
   until all the liquid is absorbed and the rice is creamy.
   Add half the reserved mushroom soaking liquid to
   the risotto and stir in the mushrooms. Season to taste
   and add more mushroom liquid, if necessary.

5 Remove the pan from the heat and stir in the
   remaining butter, grated Parmesan and chopped
   parsley. Serve immediately.

risotto with four cheeses

ingredients

serves 6

40 g/1½ oz unsalted butter

1 red onion, finely chopped

350 g/12 oz risotto rice

200 ml/7 fl oz dry white wine

1 litre/1¾ pints simmering
vegetable stock

55 g/2 oz Gorgonzola cheese,
crumbled

55 g/2 oz freshly grated
Taleggio cheese

55 g/2 oz freshly grated
fontina cheese

55 g/2 oz freshly grated
Parmesan cheese

salt and pepper

2 tbsp chopped fresh flat-leaf
parsley, to garnish

method

1 Melt the butter in a large heavy-based saucepan.
Add the onion and cook over a low heat, stirring
occasionally, for 5 minutes, until softened. Add the rice
and cook, stirring constantly, for 2–3 minutes, until all
the grains are thoroughly coated and glistening.

2 Add the wine and cook, stirring constantly, until it has
almost completely evaporated. Add a ladleful of the
hot stock and cook, stirring constantly, until all the
stock has been absorbed. Continue cooking, stirring
and adding the stock, a ladleful at a time, for about
20 minutes, or until the rice is creamy and the liquid
has been absorbed.

3 Remove the pan from the heat and stir in the
Gorgonzola, Taleggio, fontina and about one quarter
of the Parmesan until melted. Season to taste with salt
and pepper. Transfer the risotto to a warmed serving
dish, sprinkle with the remaining Parmesan, garnish
with the parsley and serve immediately.

cheese & tomato pizza

ingredients

serves 4

1 quantity pizza dough
(see page 130)
6 tomatoes, thinly sliced
175 g/6 oz mozzarella cheese,
drained and thinly sliced
2 tbsp shredded fresh basil leaves
2 tbsp olive oil
salt and pepper

method

1 To make the base, make 1 quantity of pizza dough. Turn out the proved dough onto a lightly floured work surface and knock down. Knead briefly, then roll out the dough into a circle about 5 mm/¼ inch thick. Transfer to a lightly oiled baking sheet and push up the edge with your fingers to form a small rim.

2 For the pizza topping, arrange the tomato and mozzarella slices alternately over the pizza base. Season to taste with salt and pepper, sprinkle with the basil and drizzle with the olive oil.

3 Bake in a preheated oven, 230°C/450°F/Gas Mark 8, for 15–20 minutes, until the crust is crisp and the cheese has melted. Serve immediately.

desserts

tiramisù

ingredients

serves 8

butter, for greasing
3 eggs
140 g/5 oz golden caster
    sugar
90 g/3¼ oz self-raising flour
1 tbsp cocoa powder, plus
    extra to decorate
150 ml/5 fl oz cold black
    coffee
2 tbsp rum
2 tsp cocoa powder,
    to decorate

filling

375 g/13 oz mascarpone
    cheese
225 ml/8 fl oz fresh custard
55 g/2 oz golden caster sugar
100 g/3½ oz plain chocolate,
    grated

method

1 To make the cake, grease a 20-cm/8-inch round cake tin with butter and line with baking paper. Place the eggs and sugar in a large bowl and beat together until thick and light. Sift the flour and cocoa powder over the creamed mixture and fold in gently. Spoon the cake mixture into the tin and bake in a preheated oven, 180°C/350°F/Gas Mark 4, for 30 minutes, or until the cake springs back when pressed gently in the centre. Let stand in the tin for 5 minutes, then turn out onto a wire rack to cool completely.

2 Place the black coffee and rum in a bowl or cup, mix together and set aside. To make the filling, place the mascarpone cheese in a large bowl and beat until soft. Stir in the custard, then gradually add the sugar, beating constantly. Stir in the grated chocolate.

3 Cut the cake horizontally into three layers and place one layer on a serving plate. Sprinkle with one third of the coffee mixture, then cover with one third of the mascarpone mixture. Repeat the layers, finishing with a topping of the mascarpone mixture. Chill in the refrigerator for 3 hours. Sift over the cocoa powder before serving.

zabaglione

ingredients

serves 2

4 egg yolks
60 g/2¼ oz caster sugar
75 ml/2½ fl oz Marsala
amaretti biscuits, to serve

method

1 Whisk the egg yolks with the sugar in a heatproof bowl for about 1 minute.

2 Gently whisk in the Marsala. Set the bowl over a pan of barely simmering water and whisk vigorously for 10–15 minutes, until thick, creamy and foamy.

3 Immediately pour into serving glasses and serve with amaretti biscuits.

lemon granita

ingredients

serves 4

450 ml/16 fl oz water
115 g/4 oz sugar
225 ml/8 fl oz lemon juice
grated rind of 1 lemon
lemon slices, to serve

method.

1 Heat the water in a heavy-based saucepan over a low heat. Add the sugar and stir until it has completely dissolved. Bring to the boil, remove the pan from the heat and set aside to cool completely.

2 Stir the lemon juice and rind into the syrup. Pour the mixture into a freezerproof container and place in the freezer for 3–4 hours.

3 To serve, remove the container from the freezer and dip the base into hot water. Turn out the ice block and chop roughly, then place in a food processor and process until it forms small crystals (granita means 'granular'). Spoon into glasses and serve immediately, decorated with lemon slices.

apples in white wine

ingredients

serves 4

1 kg/2 lb 4 oz apples
75 ml/2½ fl oz lemon juice
250 ml/9 fl oz white wine
200 g/7 oz sugar
1 cinnamon stick
2 cloves

method

1 Peel, quarter and core the apples. Cut them into narrow wedges and immediately sprinkle with the lemon juice.

2 Combine the wine, sugar, cinnamon stick and cloves in a saucepan and slowly bring to the boil. Add the apples and simmer on low heat for 10 minutes. Remove the apples with a slotted spoon and set them aside.

3 Bring the wine to the boil again and reduce to a thick syrup. Remove the cinnamon stick and cloves. Return the apple wedges to the pan and leave them to cool in the sauce. Serve.

cherry pie

ingredients

serves 8

500 g/1 lb 2 oz flour
150 g/5 oz caster sugar
1 pinch salt
2 eggs
grated rind of 1 orange
75 g/2¾ oz cold butter
75 g/2¾ oz lard
oil, for greasing
400 g/14 oz sour cherry jam
1 egg yolk, whisked
2 tbsp icing sugar

method

1 Sift the flour on to a work surface, mix in the sugar and make a well in the centre. Add the salt, eggs, orange rind, butter and lard and knead everything into a smooth, supple dough. Form the dough into a ball, cover it in clingfilm and chill for at least 1 hour in the refrigerator.

2 Grease a 28-cm/11-inch springform cake tin. On a floured surface, roll out two thirds of the dough very thinly and line the base and sides of the tin with it. Spread the jam evenly over the dough.

3 Roll out the remaining dough and use a pastry wheel to cut it into strips about 2 cm/¾ inch wide. Use the strips to form a lattice over the jam. Brush the top of the pie with the whisked egg yolk, then bake in a preheated oven, 180°C/350°F/Gas Mark 4, for about 45 minutes.

4 Leave the pie to cool briefly in the tin, then transfer it to a wire rack. Before serving, dust with icing sugar.

lemon pie

ingredients

serves 8

200 g/7 oz plain flour
250 g/9 oz sugar
5 egg yolks
grated rind and juice of 2 lemons
1 pinch salt
100 g/3½ oz chilled butter,
    cut into small pieces
3 eggs
150 ml/5 fl oz double cream
2 tbsp icing sugar
oil, for greasing

method

1 Sift the flour on to a work surface, mix in 100 g/3½ oz sugar and make a well in the centre. Add 4 egg yolks, half the lemon rind, the salt and the butter. Knead everything into a smooth, supple dough. Form the dough into a ball, cover it in clingfilm and chill for 1 hour in the refrigerator.

2 Lightly grease a 26-cm/10½-inch springform cake tin. On a floured surface, roll out the dough very thinly and line the base and sides of the cake tin with it. Use a fork to prick several holes in the dough, then lay a sheet of baking paper over it. Fill the pastry with dried beans and bake in a preheated oven, 180°C/350°F/Gas Mark 4, for 15 minutes. Remove the dried beans and baking paper and leave to cool.

3 Reduce the oven temperature to 160°C/325°F/Gas Mark 3. Beat the remaining egg yolk, the whole eggs and the rest of the sugar and lemon rind into a thick, pale cream. Stir in the lemon juice. Whip the cream and fold it into the egg mixture. Spread it evenly in the pastry, then bake for 20 minutes. Dust the surface with icing sugar, then return to the oven until golden brown. Leave to cool slightly, and serve.

venetian doughnuts

ingredients
serves 6

2 eggs
3 tbsp sugar
2 tsp vanilla sugar
1 pinch salt
200 g/7 oz flour
60 ml/2 fl oz olive oil
2 tbsp brandy
1 tsp grated lemon rind
oil, for deep-frying
icing sugar, for dusting

method

1 Beat the eggs with the sugar, vanilla sugar and salt until foamy. Gradually stir in the flour, olive oil, brandy and lemon peel. Leave the dough to rest for 30 minutes, then beat it vigorously once more, adding a little water or flour as needed.

2 Heat oil to 180°C/350°F in a deep frying pan or a deep-fryer. Use two teaspoons to scoop little balls of dough and drop them in the hot oil. Fry until golden brown. Place on paper towels to drain, and dust with icing sugar before serving.

chocolate & amaretto cheesecake

ingredients

serves 10–12

oil, for brushing
175 g/6 oz digestive biscuits
55 g/2 oz amaretti biscuits
85 g/3 oz butter

filling

225 g/8 oz plain chocolate,
    broken into pieces
400 g/14 oz cream cheese
115 g/4 oz golden caster sugar
3 tbsp plain flour
1 tsp vanilla extract
4 eggs
300 ml/10 fl oz double cream
50 ml/2 fl oz amaretto liqueur

topping

1 tbsp amaretto liqueur
175 g/6 oz crème fraîche
crushed amaretti biscuits

method

1 Line the base of a 23-cm/9-inch springform cake tin with foil and brush the sides with oil. Place the digestive biscuits and amaretti biscuits in a plastic bag and crush with a rolling pin. Place the butter in a saucepan and heat until just melted, then stir in the crushed biscuits. Press the mixture into the bottom of the tin and chill in the refrigerator for 1 hour.

2 To make the filling, melt the chocolate in a small heatproof bowl over a saucepan of gently simmering water, then let cool. Place the cream cheese in a bowl and beat until fluffy, then add the sugar, flour and vanilla extract and beat together until smooth. Gradually add the eggs, beating until well blended. Blend in the melted chocolate, cream and amaretto liqueur. Pour the mixture over the chilled biscuit base and bake in a preheated oven, 160°C/325°F/Gas Mark 3, for 50–60 minutes, or until set.

3 Leave the cheesecake in the oven with the door slightly ajar, until cold. Run a knife round the inside of the tin to loosen the cheesecake. Chill in the refrigerator for 2 hours, then transfer to a serving plate. To make the topping, stir the amaretto liqueur into the crème fraîche and spread over the cheesecake. Serve with a sprinkling of crushed amaretti biscuits.

ricotta cheesecake

ingredients

serves 6–8

175 g/6 oz plain flour, plus
    extra for dusting
3 tbsp caster sugar
salt
115 g/4 oz unsalted butter,
    chilled and diced
1 egg yolk

filling

450 g/1 lb ricotta cheese
125 ml/4 fl oz double cream
2 eggs, plus 1 egg yolk
85 g/3 oz caster sugar
finely grated rind of 1 lemon
finely grated rind of 1 orange

method

1 To make the pastry, sift the flour with the sugar and a pinch of salt onto a work surface and make a well in the centre. Add the diced butter and egg yolk to the well and, using your fingertips, gradually work in the flour mixture until fully incorporated. Knead very lightly.

2 Cut off about one quarter of the pastry, wrap in clingfilm and chill in the refrigerator. Press the remaining pastry into the base of a 23-cm/9-inch springform cake tin. Chill in the refrigerator for 30 minutes.

3 To make the filling, beat the ricotta with the cream, eggs and extra egg yolk, sugar, lemon rind and orange rind. Cover with clingfilm and keep cool until required.

4 Prick the base of the pastry case all over with a fork. Line with foil, fill with baking beans and bake blind in a preheated oven, 190°C/375°F/Gas Mark 5, for 15 minutes. Remove from the oven and take out the foil and beans. Stand the tin on a wire rack to cool completely.

5 Spoon the ricotta mixture into the pastry case and level the surface. Roll out the reserved pastry, cut it into strips and arrange over the filling in a lattice pattern.

6 Bake in the oven for 30–35 minutes, until the top of the cheesecake is golden and set. Cool on a wire rack before lifting off the side of the tin. Serve in wedges.

almond cake

ingredients

serves 12

3 eggs, separated
140 g/5 oz caster sugar
55 g/2 oz potato flour
140 g/5 oz almonds,
    blanched, peeled and
    finely chopped
finely grated rind of
    1 orange
125 ml/4 fl oz orange juice
salt
butter, for greasing
icing sugar, for dusting

method

1 Generously grease a round 20-cm/8-inch springform
cake tin. Beat the egg yolks with the sugar in a medium
bowl until pale and thick and the mixture leaves a
ribbon trail when the whisk is lifted. Stir in the potato
flour, almonds, orange rind and orange juice.

2 Whisk the egg whites with a pinch of salt in another
bowl until stiff. Gently fold the whites into the egg
yolk mixture.

3 Pour the mixture into the prepared tin and bake in a
preheated oven, 160°C/325°F/Gas Mark 3, for 50–60
minutes, until golden and just firm to the touch. Turn
out onto a wire rack to cool completely. Sift over a little
icing sugar to decorate before serving.

tuscan christmas cake

ingredients

serves 12–14

115 g/4 oz hazelnuts
115 g/4 oz almonds
85 g/3 oz candied peel, chopped
55 g/2 oz dried apricots,
    finely chopped
55 g/2 oz candied pineapple,
    finely chopped
grated rind of 1 orange
55 g/2 oz plain flour
2 tbsp cocoa powder
1 tsp ground cinnamon
¼ tsp ground coriander
¼ tsp freshly grated nutmeg
¼ tsp ground cloves
115 g/4 oz caster sugar
175 g/6 oz honey
icing sugar, to decorate

method

1 Line a 20-cm/8-inch springform cake tin with baking paper. Spread out the hazelnuts on a baking sheet and toast in a preheated oven, 180°C/350°F/Gas Mark 4, for 10 minutes, until golden brown. Pour them onto a tea towel and rub off the skins.

2 Meanwhile, spread out the almonds on a baking sheet and toast in the oven for 7–10 minutes, until golden. Reduce the oven temperature to 150°C/300°F/Gas Mark 2. Chop all the nuts and place in a large bowl.

3 Add the candied peel, apricots, pineapple and orange rind to the nuts and mix well. Sift the flour, cocoa powder, cinnamon, coriander, nutmeg and cloves into the bowl and mix well.

4 Put the sugar and honey in a large saucepan and stir over a low heat until the sugar has dissolved. Bring to the boil and cook for 5 minutes, until thickened. Stir in the nut and fruit mixture and remove from the heat.

5 Spoon the mixture into the prepared cake tin and level the surface. Bake in the oven for 1 hour, then transfer to a wire rack to cool completely in the tin.

6 Carefully remove the cake from the tin and peel off the baking paper. Just before serving, dredge the top with icing sugar. Cut into thin wedges to serve.

chestnut & chocolate terrine

ingredients

serves 6

200 ml/7 fl oz double cream
115 g/4 oz plain chocolate,
    melted and cooled
100 ml/3½ fl oz rum
1 packet rectangular, plain,
    sweet biscuits
225 g/8 oz canned sweetened
    chestnut purée
cocoa powder, for dusting
icing sugar, to decorate

method

1 Line a 450-g/1-lb loaf tin with clingfilm. Place the cream in a bowl and whip lightly until soft peaks form. Using a spatula, fold in the cooled chocolate.

2 Place the rum in a shallow dish. Lightly dip 4 biscuits into the rum and arrange on the bottom of the tin. Repeat with 4 more biscuits. Spread half the chocolate cream over the biscuits. Make another layer of 8 biscuits dipped in rum and spread the chestnut purée over them, followed by another layer of biscuits. Spread over the remaining chocolate cream and top with a final layer of 8 biscuits. Cover with clingfilm and chill in the refrigerator for 8 hours, or preferably overnight.

3 Turn the terrine out onto a large serving dish. Dust with cocoa powder. Cut strips of paper and place these randomly on top of the terrine. Sift over icing sugar, then carefully remove the paper. To serve, dip a sharp knife in hot water, dry it and use it to cut the terrine into slices.

italian chocolate christmas pudding

ingredients

serves 10

115 g/4 oz mixed candied
    fruit, chopped
55 g/2 oz raisins
grated rind of ½ orange
3 tbsp orange juice
3 tbsp single cream
350 g/12 oz plain
    chocolate, chopped
115 g/4 oz cream cheese
115 g/4 oz amaretti biscuits,
    roughly broken into pieces
butter, for greasing

to serve

125 ml/4 fl oz whipping cream
2 tbsp amaretto liqueur
25 g/1 oz plain chocolate, grated

method

1 Place the candied fruit, raisins, orange rind and juice in a bowl and mix together. Put the single cream and chocolate in a saucepan and heat gently until the chocolate has melted. Stir until smooth, then stir in the fruit mixture. Remove the pan from the heat and set aside to cool.

2 Lightly grease an 850-ml/1½ pint ovenproof bowl with butter. Place the cream cheese and a little of the chocolate mixture in a large bowl and beat together until smooth, then stir in the remaining chocolate mixture. Stir in the broken amaretti biscuits. Pour into the prepared bowl, cover with clingfilm and chill in the refrigerator overnight.

3 To serve, turn the pudding out onto a chilled serving plate. Pour the whipping cream into a bowl and add the amaretto liqueur. Whip lightly until slightly thickened. Pour some of the cream over the pudding and sprinkle grated chocolate over the top. Serve with the remaining cream.

mascarpone creams

ingredients

serves 4

115 g/4 oz amaretti biscuits,
    crushed
60 ml/2 fl oz amaretto
    or Maraschino
4 eggs, separated
55 g/2 oz caster sugar
225 g/8 oz mascarpone cheese
toasted flaked almonds,
    to decorate

method

1 Place the amaretti crumbs in a bowl, add the amaretto
    or Maraschino and set aside to soak.

2 Meanwhile, beat the egg yolks with the caster sugar
    until pale and thick. Fold in the mascarpone and
    soaked biscuit crumbs.

3 Whisk the egg whites in a separate, spotlessly clean
    bowl until stiff, then gently fold into the cheese
    mixture. Divide the mascarpone cream between
    4 serving dishes and chill in the refrigerator for
    1–2 hours. Sprinkle with the flaked almonds just
    before serving.

chilled chocolate dessert

ingredients

serves 4-6

225 g/8 oz mascarpone cheese
2 tbsp finely ground coffee beans
25 g/1 oz icing sugar
85 g/3 oz unsweetened chocolate, finely grated
350 ml/12 fl oz double cream, plus extra to decorate
Marsala, to serve

method

1 Beat the mascarpone cheese with the coffee and icing sugar until thoroughly combined.

2 Set aside 4 teaspoons of the grated chocolate and stir the remainder into the cheese mixture with 75 ml/2½ fl oz of the unwhipped cream.

3 Whisk the remaining cream until it forms soft peaks. Stir 1 tablespoon of the cream into the mascarpone mixture to slacken it, then fold the cream into the remaining mascarpone mixture using a figure-of-eight action to blend it in.

4 Spoon the mixture into a freezerproof container and place in the freezer for about 3 hours.

5 To serve, scoop the chocolate dessert into sundae glasses and drizzle with a little Marsala. Top with the extra cream, whipped, and decorate with the reserved grated chocolate. Serve immediately.

cappuccino soufflé puddings

ingredients

serves 4

2 tbsp golden caster sugar,
plus extra for coating

90 ml/3 fl oz whipping cream

2 tsp instant espresso coffee
granules

2 tbsp Kahlúa

3 large eggs, separated,
plus 1 extra egg white

150 g/5½ oz plain chocolate,
melted and cooled

butter, for greasing

cocoa powder, for dusting

vanilla ice cream, to serve

method

1 Lightly grease the sides of 4 x 175-ml/6-fl oz ramekins
with butter and coat with caster sugar. Place the
ramekins on a baking sheet.

2 Place the cream in a small, heavy-based saucepan and
heat gently. Stir in the coffee until it has dissolved, then
stir in the Kahlúa. Divide the coffee mixture between
the prepared ramekins.

3 Place the egg whites in a clean, greasefree bowl and
whisk until soft peaks form, then gradually whisk in
the sugar until stiff but not dry. Stir the egg yolks and
melted chocolate together in a separate bowl, then stir
in a little of the whisked egg whites. Gradually fold in
the remaining egg whites.

4 Divide the mixture between the dishes. Bake in
a preheated oven, 190°C/375°F/Gas Mark 5, for
15 minutes, or until just set. Dust with cocoa and
serve immediately with vanilla ice cream.

coffee panna cotta
with chocolate sauce

ingredients

serves 6

oil, for brushing
600 ml/1 pint double cream
1 vanilla pod
55 g/2 oz golden caster sugar
2 tsp instant espresso coffee
  granules, dissolved in
  60 ml/2 fl oz water
2 tsp powdered gelatine

sauce

150 ml/5 fl oz single cream
55 g/2 oz plain chocolate, melted

to decorate

chocolate-covered coffee beans
cocoa, for dusting

method

1 Lightly brush 6 x 150-ml/5-fl oz moulds with oil. Place the cream in a saucepan. Split the vanilla pod and scrape the black seeds into the cream. Add the vanilla pod and the sugar, then heat gently until almost boiling. Sieve the cream into a heatproof bowl and reserve. Place the coffee in a small heatproof bowl, sprinkle on the gelatine and leave for 5 minutes, or until spongy. Set the bowl over a saucepan of gently simmering water until the gelatine has dissolved.

2 Stir a little of the reserved cream into the gelatine mixture, then stir the gelatine mixture into the remainder of the cream. Divide the mixture between the prepared moulds and cool, then chill in the refrigerator for 8 hours, or overnight.

3 To make the sauce, place one quarter of the cream in a bowl and stir in the melted chocolate. Gradually stir in the remaining cream, reserving 1 tablespoon. To serve the panna cotta, dip the bases of the moulds briefly into hot water and turn out onto 6 dessert plates. Pour the chocolate cream around. Dot drops of the reserved cream onto the sauce and feather it with a skewer. Decorate with chocolate-covered coffee beans and cocoa. Serve immediately.

index